ENGLISH G

| G9 |

access 5

VOKABELTASCHENBUCH

W0214149

Cornelsen

Hier siehst du, wie das **Vocabulary** aufgebaut ist:

Diese Zahl gibt die **Seite** an, auf der die Wörter zum ersten Mal vorkommen. pp. 12/13 = Seiten 12 und 13

Die **Lautschrift** zeigt dir, wie ein Wort ausgesprochen wird. Eine Übersicht über alle **Lautschriftzeichen** findest du auf S. 4.

pp. 12/13 **coastal** ['kəʊstl]	Küsten-	Plymouth is a ~ town in England.
kangaroo [ˌkæŋgə'ruː] (*AusE infml:* **roo**)	Känguru	! stress: **kangaroo** [ˌkæŋgə'ruː]
humid ['hjuːmɪd]	feucht, feuchtwarm	We get a lot of rain here in the summer, so it's often very ~. (F) humide (L) umidus **humid** ◄► **dry**
…t]	abgelegen, abgeschieden	We stayed in a ~ village 60 … town.
	sandig	noun: **sand** – adj: **sandy**
	Kamel	! stress: **camel** ['kæml]
convict ['kɒnvɪkt]	Sträfling, Strafgefangene(r)	
poisonous ['pɔɪzənəs]	giftig	Be careful! Snakes can be ~. If you eat ~ plants, you might die.
flying fox [ˌflaɪɪŋ 'fɒks]	Flughund	 a **flying fox** 
fox [fɒks]	Fuchs	

Die Tilde in den Beispielsätzen steht für das neue Wort.
poisonous – If you eat ~ plants, … (= … **poisonous** plants)

Eingerückte Wörter lernst du am besten zusammen mit dem vorausgehenden Wort, weil die beiden zusammengehören.

Das **rote Ausrufezeichen** bedeutet: Vorsicht, hier macht man leicht Fehler!

p. 21 **(to) argue – argument – argumentative**

• (to) **argue**	1. argumentieren; behaupten 2. (sich) streiten, (sich) zanken	He tried to **argue** that Shakespeare was German! My brothers **argue** all the time.
• **argument**	1. Argument 2. Streit, Auseinandersetzung	Try to present **arguments** for and against the topic. Sorry about the noise. Our neighbours are having another **argument**.
• **argumentative** [ˌɑːgju'mentətɪv]	1. argumentativ 2. streitsüchtig	**argumentative writing** (Erörterung, Argumentation) He's a bit **argumentative**. That's why he didn't agree with us.

viele Ideen wie … We sat down and **~ed** on how to solve the problem.

Diese **Kästen** solltest du dir immer besonders gut ansehen: Hier sind Vokabeln zu einem bestimmten Thema zusammengestellt. Oder du erfährst mehr über ein Wort und wie es verwendet wird.

Dies ist das *„opposite"*-Zeichen („Gegenteil"-Zeichen): **humid** und **dry** sind *opposites*.

Im **Vocabulary** werden folgende **Abkürzungen** verwendet:

p. = page (Seite)	pp. = pages (Seiten)
sth. = something (etwas)	sb. = somebody (jemand)
jn. = jemanden	jm. = jemandem

pl = *plural* (Mehrzahl) *adj* = *adjective* *adv* = *adverb* *conj* = *conjunction* *prep* = *preposition*

BE = *British English* *AE* = *American English* *AusE* = *Australian English*

infml = *informal* (umgangssprachlich) *fml* = *formal* (formell, förmlich)

Ⓕ = *verwandtes Wort im Französischen* Ⓛ = *verwandtes Wort im Lateinischen*

- Eine Übersicht über alle **Lautschriftzeichen** und das englische **Alphabet** findest du auf S. 4.
- Eine Liste der **unregelmäßigen Verben** steht auf den Seiten 94–98.

English sounds

[iː]	green, he, sea
[i]	happy, monkey
[ɪ]	big, in, expensive
[e]	red, yes, again, breakfast
[æ]	cat, animal, apple, black
[ɑː]	class, ask, car, park
[ɒ]	song, on, dog, what
[ɔː]	door, or, ball, four, morning
[uː]	blue, ruler, too, two, you
[ʊ]	book, good, pullover
[ʌ]	mum, bus, colour
[ɜː]	girl, early, her, work, T-shirt
[ə]	a partner, again, today

[eɪ]	name, eight, play, great
[aɪ]	time, right, my, I
[ɔɪ]	boy, toilet, noise
[əʊ]	old, no, road, yellow
[aʊ]	town, now, house
[ɪə]	here, year, idea
[eə]	where, pair, share, their
[ʊə]	tour

[b]	boat, table, verb
[p]	pool, paper, shop
[d]	dad, window, good
[t]	ten, letter, at
[g]	good, again, bag
[k]	cat, kitchen, back
[m]	mum, man, remember
[n]	no, one, ten
[ŋ]	song, young, uncle, thanks
[l]	hello, like, old, small
[r]	red, ruler, friend, sorry
[w]	we, where, one
[j]	you, yes, uniform
[f]	family, after, laugh
[v]	river, very, seven, have
[s]	sister, poster, yes
[z]	please, zoo, quiz, his, music
[ʃ]	shop, station, English
[ʒ]	television, usually
[tʃ]	teacher, child, watch
[dʒ]	Germany, job, project, orange
[θ]	thanks, three, bathroom
[ð]	the, this, father, with
[h]	here, who, behind
[x]	loch

The English alphabet

a	[eɪ]	**n**	[en]
b	[biː]	**o**	[əʊ]
c	[siː]	**p**	[piː]
d	[diː]	**q**	[kjuː]
e	[iː]	**r**	[ɑː]
f	[ef]	**s**	[es]
g	[dʒiː]	**t**	[tiː]
h	[eɪtʃ]	**u**	[juː]
i	[aɪ]	**v**	[viː]
j	[dʒeɪ]	**w**	[ˈdʌbljuː]
k	[keɪ]	**x**	[eks]
l	[el]	**y**	[waɪ]
m	[em]	**z**	[zed]

Am besten kannst du dir die Aussprache der einzelnen Lautzeichen einprägen, wenn du dir zu jedem Zeichen ein einfaches Wort merkst – das [iː] ist der **green**-Laut, das [eɪ] ist der **name**-Laut usw.

The English-speaking world

pp. 10/11	**independent** [ˌɪndɪˈpendənt]	unabhängig	Australia became ~ from Britain in 1901. (F) indépendant/e
	dependency [dɪˈpendənsi]	Schutzgebiet, Kolonie	a region/a country controlled by another country
	incredible [ɪnˈkredəbl]	unglaublich	That's ~! I don't believe it! (F) incroyable (L) incredibilis
	statistics *(pl)* [stəˈtɪstɪks]	Statistik	**Statistics** show that about 360 million people speak English as their first language. (F) les statistiques a **key statistic** = eine statistische Schlüsselkennzahl
	populous [ˈpɒpjələs]	bevölkerungsreich; dicht besiedelt	a ~ area = an area where a lot of people live
	billion [ˈbɪljən]	Milliarde *(tausend Millionen)*	
	Hindi [ˈhɪndi]	Hindi	one of the languages spoken in India
	(to) **represent** [ˌreprɪˈzent]	vertreten, repräsentieren; verkörpern, symbolisieren	A group of people from Bonn **~ed** Germany. A red heart usually **~s** love. verb: (to) **represent** – noun: **representative** [ˌreprɪˈzentətɪv] (Vertreter/in, Repräsentant/in)

Unit 1 Australia

pp. 12/13	**coastal** ['kəʊstl]	Küsten-	Plymouth is a ~ town in England.
	bush [bʊʃ]	Busch, Strauch *(auch: unerschlossenes, „wildes" Land in Australien u. Afrika)*	
	coral ['kɒrəl]	Koralle; Korallen-	! stress: **co̲ral** ['kɒrəl]
	kangaroo [ˌkæŋgə'ruː] (*AusE infml:* **roo**)	Känguru	! stress: **kanga̲r̲o̲o̲** [ˌkæŋgə'ruː]
	the outback ['aʊtbæk]	das Hinterland Australiens	
	spider ['spaɪdə]	Spinne	**spiders**
	humid ['hjuːmɪd]	feucht, feuchtwarm	We get a lot of rain here in the summer, so it's often very ~. (F) humide (L) umidus **humid ◄► dry**
	remote [rɪ'məʊt]	abgelegen, abgeschieden	We stayed in a ~ village 60 miles from the nearest town. (L) remotus
	sandy ['sændi]	sandig	noun: **sand** – adj: **sandy**

stunning ['stʌnɪŋ]	atemberaubend, überwältigend, umwerfend	= wonderful, amazing, fantastic Don't they look ~ in their wedding clothes? 
urban ['ɜːbən]	städtisch, Stadt-	**Urban** planners think about the future of towns and cities. (F) urbain, e (L) urbanus
Aboriginal [ˌæbə'rɪdʒənl]	Aborigine- *(die Ureinwohner/-innen Australiens betreffend)*	~ artists/culture; the ~ population the **Aboriginal** flag 
camel ['kæml]	Kamel	! stress: **<u>ca</u>mel** ['kæml]
convict ['kɒnvɪkt]	Sträfling, Strafgefangene(r)	
koala [kəʊ'ɑːlə]	Koala	a **koala** 
poisonous ['pɔɪzənəs]	giftig	Be careful! Snakes can be ~. If you eat ~ plants, you might die.
territory ['terətri]	Territorium, Revier	(F) le territoire (L) terra, -ae *f* (*Erde, Land*)

Part A

p. 14	**flight** [flaɪt]	Flug	verb: (to) **fly, flew, flown** – noun: **flight** an **in-flight** magazine/meal = ein Bordmagazin/eine Bordmahlzeit
	circular ['sɜːkjələ]	kreisförmig, rund	noun: **circle** – adj: **circular**
	quay [kiː]	Kai	! pronunciation: **quay** ['kiː] Ⓕ le quai
	(to) **settle** ['setl]	sich niederlassen, sich ansiedeln	When the Romans **~d** in Britain, they built roads and towns.
	trendy ['trendi]	modisch, angesagt, „in“	Everyone is talking about this ~ new restaurant in George Street.
	suburb ['sʌbɜːb]	Vorort	It's so noisy in the town centre that we have decided to move to a ~. Ⓛ sub (*unter*),urbs *f* (*Stadt*)
	wharf [wɔːf]	Kai, Anlegeplatz	a place for boats next to the sea or a river
	botanic [bə'tænɪk]	botanisch	
	business ['bɪznəs]	Geschäft, Geschäfts-; Unternehmen, Betrieb	**Business** was good. (Die Geschäfte liefen gut.) a ~ trip/lunch (Geschäftsreise/-essen) Mike started his own ~ when he was 17.
	district ['dɪstrɪkt]	Gegend, Bezirk, Viertel	There are lots of skyscrapers in Sydney's business ~.

flying fox [ˌflaɪɪŋ ˈfɒks]	Flughund	 a **flying fox**
fox [fɒks]	Fuchs	a **fox** 
opera [ˈɒprə]	Oper	(F) l'opéra (*m*)
(to) **beg (for)** [beg]	betteln (um)	Don't feed the pigeons – even if they ~ **for** food.
waterfront [ˈwɔːtəfrʌnt]	Hafenviertel *(oft modernisiert und zum Wohnviertel umgebaut)*	
contemporary [kənˈtemprəri]	zeitgenössisch	~ art/music/dance/literature
(to) **guide** [gaɪd]	führen	verb: (to) **guide** adj: **guided** – a **guided tour** through the city noun: **guide** **1.** Fremdenführer/in; Reiseleiter/in; **2.** (*auch:* **guidebook**) Reiseführer
honest [ˈɒnɪst]	ehrlich	Be ~ with me! Say what you really think. ! silent "**h**": **honest** [ˈɒnɪst] (L) honestus
take (on sth.)	Einstellung, Meinung (zu etwas)	What's your ~ **on** this new band?
scenic [ˈsiːnɪk]	(landschaftlich) schön	Let's take the ~ coastal route, not the main road.
(to) **transform** [trænsˈfɔːm]	verwandeln; umwandeln	They're planning to ~ the station into an art gallery. (F) transformer (L) transformare
landmark [ˈlændmɑːk]	Wahrzeichen	St Paul's Cathedral is one of London's **~s.**

paradise ['pærədaɪs]	Paradies	! stress: **paradise** ['pærədaɪs]	(F) le paradis
p. 15 **testimonial** [ˌtestɪ'məʊniəl]	Erfahrungsbericht; Zeugnis		
destination [ˌdestɪ'neɪʃn]	(Reise-)Ziel, Bestimmungsort	Majorca is a popular holiday ~.	(F) la destination
(to) **apply (for** sth.**)** [ə'plaɪ]	sich (um/für etwas) bewerben	He **applied for** the job, but he didn't get it. I think it's better to ~ to more than one university.	
(to) **contact** sb. ['kɒntækt]	Kontakt zu jm. aufnehmen, sich bei jm. melden	noun: **contact** – verb: (to) **contact** ! stress: **contact** ['kɒntækt]	(F) contacter (L) contingere
Aussie ['ɒzi] *(infml)*	Australier/in; australisch	informal for "Australian"	
though [ðəʊ]	obwohl	Leon really liked his host family, ~ (= although) it was hard to understand them at first.	
especially [ɪ'speʃli]	besonders, vor allem	I love chocolate, ~ chocolate from Belgium.	
barbecue ['bɑːbɪkjuː] *(BE und AusE infml auch:* **barbie;** Abkürzung: **BBQ)**	Grill; Grillfest, Grillparty	Shall I put some more sausages on the ~? We're having a ~ on Sunday. Would you like to come?	
(to) **swallow** ['swɒləʊ]	schlucken; verschlucken	He thought he was going to be sick when he realized that he had **~ed** a spider.	
ton [tʌn]	Tonne *(Gewicht)*	It was so hot! We sold **~s** of ice cream. (jede Menge)	

private ['praɪvət]	privat	! pronunciation and stress: **private** ['praɪvət] **private** ◄► **public** (F) privé, e (L) privatus, -a, -um
(to) **accept** [ək'sept]	akzeptieren, annehmen	I asked eight people to our barbecue, and they all **~ed** the invitation. (F) accepter (L) accipere As a child, I found it hard to get **~ed** into a group.
talkative ['tɔːkətɪv]	gesprächig	He seemed shy at first, but later he got really ~.
photography [fə'tɒgrəfi]	Fotografie	! stress: **photography** [fə'tɒgrəfi] (F) la photographie
(to) **be/get homesick** ['həʊmsɪk]	Heimweh haben/bekommen	*English:* (to) **be homesick** *German:* **Heimweh haben**
self-confident [ˌself'kɒnfɪdənt] (*kurz auch:* **confident**)	selbstbewusst, (selbst)sicher	She's a **self-confident** student. As a child, I was very shy. Later I became more **confident.** (L) confidere (*vertrauen*)
easy-going [ˌiːzi'gəʊɪŋ]	locker, unbeschwert, gelassen	Our arts teacher is **easy-~**, but Mr Hall is very strict.

Adjektive, die aus mehr als einem Wort bestehen

Adjektive, die aus mehr als einem Wort bestehen, werden in der Regel mit Bindestrich geschrieben:

a self-confident girl	selbstbewusst, (selbst)sicher	**an easy-going boy**	locker, unbeschwert, gelassen
English-speaking countries	englischsprachig	**a user-friendly program**	(be)nutzerfreundlich
a well-known singer	bekannt, berühmt	**open-minded parents**	aufgeschlossen, offen, tolerant
a family-owned company	familiengeführt	**a three-week holiday**	dreiwöchig

	way of life [ˌweɪ‿əv 'laɪf]	Lebensweise, Lebensart	
p. 16	**general** ['dʒenrəl]	allgemeine(r, s)	(F) général, e
	statement ['steɪtmənt]	Aussage; Erklärung; Aussagesatz	
	in progress ['prəʊgres]	im Gange, im Verlauf	You can't go in, there's a meeting **in ~.** (L) progredi (*voranschreiten*)
	sunscreen ['sʌnskriːn]	Sonnenschutzmittel	Put on ~ before you go out in the sun.
p. 17	**No worries, mate.** ['wʌriz] *(bes. AusE)*	Kein Problem! / Alles OK! / Alles gut!	Thanks very much for helping me. – **No ~, mate.**
	intonation [ˌɪntə'neɪʃn]	Intonation; Satzmelodie	Questions usually have a rising ~. (F) l'intonation (*f*)
	(to) **rise** [raɪz]**, rose** [rəʊz], **risen** ['rɪzən]	(an)steigen, aufsteigen; (sich) erhöhen	It is getting warmer. Temperatures are **rising.** Food prices have **risen** again. Clouds of smoke **rose** from the building. verb: (to) **rise, rose, risen** – noun: **rise** (Erhöhung, Anstieg)
	pitch [pɪtʃ]	Tonlage, Tonhöhe	
	(to) **tend to be/do** sth. [tend]	dazu neigen etwas zu tun/sein, meistens etwas tun/sein	When I like a place very much, I ~ **to** spend every holiday there. (= I usually spend …)

among [ə'mʌŋ]	zwischen, unter *(mehreren Personen, Tieren, Dingen)*	 **among** the boys  **between** the boys
unsure [ˌʌn'ʃʊə], [ˌʌn'ʃɔː]	unsicher	**sure** ◄► **unsure**
sb. **lacks** sth. [læks]	jm. fehlt es an etwas	He didn't get the job because he **~ed** experience. verb: (to) **lack** – noun: **lack (of)** (Mangel (an))
confidence ['kɒnfɪdəns]	(Selbst-)Vertrauen, Zuversicht	adj: **confident** – noun: **confidence** (F) la confiance (L) confidentia
(to) **pay attention** (to) [ə'tenʃn]	achten (auf), aufpassen (auf)	Stop talking now and **pay ~,** please. **attention** = Aufmerksamkeit (F) l'attention *(f)* "Ladies and gentlemen, may I have your ~, please."
(to) **distract** [dɪ'strækt]	ablenken	verb: (to) **distract** – noun: **distraction** [dɪ'strækʃn] (Ablenkung)

p. 18

any – anybody/anyone – anything – anywhere

- The words **any, anybody** (or **anyone**), **anything** and **anywhere** are used in **questions** and **negative statements:**

Questions:		Negative statements:
Are there **any** buses after midnight?		I don't need **any** help with this.
Do you know **anybody/anyone** here?		I do**n't** know **anybody/anyone** here.
Do you need **anything** from the shops?		She didn't say **anything.**
Have you seen my keys **anywhere?**		I ca**n't** find my shoes **anywhere.**

- They can also be used **in positive statements,** but then the meaning is different:

You'll get that book in **any** bookshop.	*in jedem (beliebigen) Buchladen*
Anybody/Anyone looking for cheap CDs should try this shop.	*jeder; alle*
I guess **anything** is better than having to sit at home.	*alles*
Accidents can happen **anywhere.**	*überall*

several ['sevrəl]	mehrere, verschiedene	There are ~ shops round here that sell cold drinks.
p. 19 **section** ['sekʃn]	Teil(stück), Abschnitt	This ~ of the road is quite dangerous. (F) la section
back and forth [fɔːθ]	hin und her; hin und zurück; auf und ab	There's a small train that runs **back and** ~ between the two villages.
skin [skɪn]	Haut	I need some face cream. My ~ is very dry.
sunburn ['sʌnbɜːn]	Sonnenbrand	Put on sunscreen to protect your skin from ~.

p. 21

(to) argue – argument – argumentative

• (to) **argue**	**1.** argumentieren; behaupten **2.** (sich) streiten, (sich) zanken	He tried to **argue** that Shakespeare was German! My brothers **argue** all the time.
• **Argument**	**1.** Argument **2.** Streit, Auseinandersetzung	Try to present **arguments** for and against the topic. Sorry about the noise. Our neighbours are having another **argument**.
• **argumentative** [ˌɑːgjuˈmentətɪv]	**1.** argumentativ **2.** streitsüchtig	**argumentative writing** (Erörterung, Argumentation) He's a bit **argumentative.** That's why he didn't agree with us.

(to) **brainstorm** [ˈbreɪnstɔːm]	brainstormen *(so viele Ideen wie möglich sammeln)*	We sat down and **~ed** on how to solve the problem.
(to) **oppose** sth. [əˈpəʊz]	etwas ablehnen, gegen etwas sein	Most people **~d** the plan to build a new road. (to) **support** sth. ◄► (to) **oppose** sth. Ⓛ opponere *(entgegenstellen)*
abroad [əˈbrɔːd]	im/ins Ausland	My great-grandparents have never been ~. Lots of people like to go ~ on holiday.
in addition [əˈdɪʃn]	zusätzlich, außerdem, darüber hinaus	Our new coffee machine uses less energy. **In** ~, it's very easy to clean. **In** ~ to the guitar, he also plays the piano. Ⓛ addere *(hinzufügen)*
(to) **state** sth. [steɪt]	etwas äußern, etwas angeben	Try to ~ your opinion in a respectful way. The president **~d** that he would introduce a new law.

briefly ['briːfli]	in Kürze, in wenigen Worten	Don't go into detail. Just explain ~. (F) brièvement (L) brevis, -e (*kurz*)
personally ['pɜːsənəli]	persönlich	*English:* **Personally,** I'd rather go by train. *German:* Ich **persönlich** würde lieber mit dem Zug fahren.
(to) **discuss** sth. [dɪ'skʌs]	über etwas diskutieren, etwas besprechen	*English:* (to) **discuss** sth. *German:* **über etwas diskutieren** noun: **discussion** – verb: (to) **discuss** sth.
furthermore [ˌfɜːðə'mɔː]	außerdem, ferner; des Weiteren	The government want to improve our hospitals. **Furthermore,** they have promised to spend more on education.
in my view [vjuː]	meiner Ansicht nach, meiner Meinung nach	= in my opinion
On the one hand, … **On the other hand, …**	Einerseits … Andererseits …	**On the one** ~, Australia is close to Asia. **On the other** ~, it has a strong British tradition.
(to) **take a different view**	einen anderen Standpunkt vertreten; anderer Ansicht sein	Most people think it's OK to eat meat, but some **take a different** ~. Some people **took the view that** the new skyscraper destroyed the historical skyline. („… waren der Auffassung/Ansicht, dass …")

comparison [kəm'pærɪsn]	Vergleich	On this website you can **make ~s** between different schools. (F) la comparaison (L) comparare *English:* (to) **make comparisons** *German:* **Vergleiche anstellen; vergleichen** verb: (to) **compare** – noun: **comparison**
In the first place, …	Erstens …; Zunächst …	**In the first** ~, we need to contact the head teacher.
Firstly, … ['fɜːstli] **Secondly, …** ['sekəndli] **Thirdly, …** ['θɜːdli]	Erstens … Zweitens … Drittens …	**Firstly,** we have to get something to drink. **Secondly,** we need a DJ. And **thirdly, …**

Part B

pp. 22/23

cape [keɪp]	Kap	a piece of land that sticks out into the sea
reef [riːf]	Riff	Coral **~s** all over the world are in danger.
wet [wet]	Nässe	adj: **wet** – noun: **wet**
folk *(pl)* [fəʊk] *(infml)*	Leute	The ~ round here aren't very friendly to tourists.
season ['siːzn]	Jahreszeit; Saison	*English:* **busy season** *German:* **Hauptsaison**
(to) **be determined to do** sth. [dɪ'tɜːmɪnd]	(fest) entschlossen sein, etwas zu tun	Nothing will stop me: **I'm ~ to** win the race. (L) determinare
cyclone ['saɪkləʊn]	Zyklon, Wirbelsturm	

insect ['ɪnsekt]	Insekt	! stress: **insect** ['ɪnsekt] (F) l'insecte (*m*)
python ['paɪθən]	Python	! pronunciation: **python** ['paɪθən]
luckily ['lʌkɪli]	glücklicherweise; zum Glück	I dropped a plate yesterday. **Luckily,** it wasn't very expensive.
human ['hjuːmən]	Mensch; menschlich	! **human** = **1.** Mensch – animals and **humans** **2.** menschlich – It's only **human.** *Für „Mensch" wird oft auch* **human being** *verwendet:* The earth is older than **human beings.** (F) humain, e (L) humanus
(to) **feed on** [fiːd], **fed, fed** [fed]	sich ernähren von	! (to) **feed** = **1.** füttern; **2.** sich ernähren
mainly ['meɪnli]	hauptsächlich, vorwiegend	The hotel was full of tourists, ~ from Germany.
(to) **provoke** [prə'vəʊk]	provozieren	He's an easy-going guy – it's difficult to ~ him. (F) provoquer (L) provocare
(to) **injure** sb. ['ɪndʒə]	jn. verletzen	! Bei leichten körperlichen Verletzungen oder wenn Gefühle verletzt werden, wird eher **hurt** verwendet.
moth [mɒθ]	Nachtfalter; Motte	a **moth** 

	crocodile ['krɒkədaɪl] (*infml auch:* **croc**)	Krokodil	**!** pronunciation and stress: **crocodile** ['krɒkədaɪl]
	(to) **bump into** sb. [bʌmp] *(infml)*	jn. Zufällig treffen, jm. zufällig begegnen	In a small town, you often ~ **into** people you know.
	(to) **snorkel** ['snɔːkl]	schnorcheln	**snorkelling** 
p. 24	**greenhouse** ['griːnhaʊs]	Gewächshaus, Treibhaus	a **greenhouse** 
p. 25	(to) **shorten** ['ʃɔːtn]	(ver)kürzen	adj: **short** – verb: (to) **shorten**
	formal ['fɔːml]	formell, förmlich	**formal** ◄► **informal** [ɪn'fɔːml] (informell; umgangssprachlich) Ⓕ formel, le ◄► informel, le
	the tropics *(pl)* ['trɒpɪks]	die Tropen	
p. 26	**coastline** ['kəʊstlaɪn]	Küste, Küstenlinie	From the boat we could see the rocky Irish ~.
	entertainment [ˌentə'teɪnmənt]	Unterhaltung *(Belustigung, Vergnügen)*	There's usually lots of ~ on a cruise ship: films, shows, concerts, etc.
	facilities *(pl)* [fə'sɪlətiz]	Einrichtungen, Ausstattung, Anlage(n), Angebot(e)	The ~ at the first hotel were much better than the ones in this place! Ⓛ facilis

overcrowded [ˌəʊvəˈkraʊdɪd]	überfüllt	~ streets/beaches/classrooms/cities/prisons
rural [ˈrʊərəl]	ländlich, Land-	**rural ◀▶ urban** (F) rural, e ◀▶ urbain, e (L) rus, ruris n (*Land*)
suburban [səˈbɜːbən]	Vorort-, Vorstadt-; vorstädtisch	He walked around the ~ streets taking photos of the houses and gardens. noun: **suburb** [ˈsʌbɜːb] – adj: **suburban**
inland [ˈɪnlænd]	Binnen-; im Landesinneren	Duisburg has the world's largest ~ harbour. **coastal ◀▶ inland**
mild [maɪld]	mild	a **mild climate** ◀▶ a **tropical climate** a **mild dish/sauce** ◀▶ a **hot dish/sauce** a **mild cheese** ◀▶ a **strong cheese** ! pronunciation: **mild** [maɪld]
mountainous [ˈmaʊntənəs]	bergig, gebirgig	noun: **mountain** – adj: **mountainous**
old-fashioned [ˌəʊldˈfæʃənd]	altmodisch	**old-fashioned ◀▶ modern, trendy**
southern [ˈsʌðən]	südlich, Süd-	**north – northern** **south – southern** **east – eastern** **west – western** ! pronunciation: **south** [saʊθ] – **southern** [ˈsʌðən]
tiny [ˈtaɪni]	winzig	**tiny ◀▶ huge**

collocation [ˌkɒləˈkeɪʃn]	Kollokation *(Wörter, die oft zusammen vorkommen)*	words that are often used together, for example • **strong wind** (starker/kräftiger Wind) • **heavy rain** (starker/heftiger Regen) (F) la collocation (L) collocare
descriptive [dɪˈskrɪptɪv]	beschreibend	verb: (to) **describe** – (L) describere noun: **description** [dɪˈskrɪpʃn] (Beschreibung) – adj: **descriptive**
p. 27 (to) **disagree (with)** [ˌdɪsəˈgriː]	anderer Meinung sein (als); nicht übereinstimmen (mit); nicht zustimmen	I'm sorry, but I completely ~ **with** you/**with** that statement. (to) **agree** ◄► (to) **disagree**
nonsense [ˈnɒnsns]	Unsinn, dummes Zeug	
direct [dəˈrekt], [daɪˈrekt]	direkt	**direct** ◄► **indirect** [ˌɪndəˈrekt], [ˌɪndaɪˈrekt]
hurtful [ˈhɜːtfl]	verletzend	a ~ comment = a comment that hurts/might hurt
I'm afraid … [əˈfreɪd]	Leider …	 **! afraid: 1. I'm afraid of spiders.** (Ich habe Angst …) **2. I'm afraid I can't help you.** (Leider …)

(to) **have a point**	nicht ganz Unrecht haben	You **have a** ~ there, but I still think the other arguments are better.
gift voucher ['gɪft vaʊtʃə]	Geschenkgutschein	I got a couple of **gift ~s** for my birthday.

Part C

p. 30 (to) **dig (for** sth.**)** [dɪg], **dug, dug** [dʌg]	(nach etwas) graben	**digging a hole** 

English "So" – German "auch"

Coreen loves talking about her culture, and **so do** the other kids. … und die anderen Kids **auch.**

Mit **so** + **Hilfsverb** + **(Pro-)Nomen** kann man zum Ausdruck bringen, dass etwas **auch** für jemand anders gilt. Weitere Beispiele:

John **is** really clever.	**So is** Joanna.	He **has been** to Australia.	**So has** Joanna.
He **has got** a great voice.	**So has** Joanna.	He **got** married last year.	**So did** Joanna.
He **can** speak several languages.	**So can** Joanna.	He **would like** to move to Spain.	**So would** Joanna.
He **earns** a lot of money.	**So does** Joanna.		

(to) **camp (out)** [kæmp]	zelten, im Freien kampieren	
(to) **dream** [driːm]	träumen	verb: (to) **dream** – noun: **dream**
painting ['peɪntɪŋ]	Gemälde, Bild	verb: (to) **paint** – noun: **painting**

sort (of) [sɔːt]	Art, Sorte	What ~ **of** music do you like? Rock? (= What kind of music …)
fewer ['fjuːə]	weniger	Only three mistakes? That's ~ than I expected.

German "wenig, weniger, am wenigsten"

1. *mit dem Plural von zählbaren Nomen:*	**a few bottles/coins**	**fewer bottles/coins**	**the fewest bottles/coins**
2. *mit nicht zählbaren Nomen:*	**a little milk/money**	**less milk/money**	**the least milk/money**

	opportunity [ˌɒpə'tjuːnəti]	Gelegenheit, Möglichkeit, Chance	I think you'll have better job **opportunities** if you spend a year abroad. (L) opportunus
	work experience *(no pl)* ['wɜːk‿ɪkˌspɪəriəns]	Arbeitserfahrung(en), Praxiserfahrung(en); Praktikum	She has a strong computer background and a lot of **work ~**. Last summer I did some **work ~** at a local shop.
	health [helθ]	Gesundheit	
	clinic ['klɪnɪk]	Klinik	(F) la clinique
	patient ['peɪʃnt]	Patient/in	! pronunciation and stress: **patient** ['peɪʃnt] (L) pati *(leiden)*
	community [kə'mjuːnəti]	Gemeinde; Gemeinschaft	Bayern Munich has a big ~ of fans all over Germany. (L) communis, -e (gemeinsam)
p. 31	(to) **debate** sth. [dɪ'beɪt]	über etwas debattieren	We **~d** the topic of bringing mobiles to school. verb: (to) **debate** – noun: **debate** (Debatte)

racism ['reɪsɪzm]	Rassismus	! stress: **racism** ['reɪsɪzm] **racist** ['reɪsɪst] (F) le racisme (F) le/la raciste
racist ['reɪsɪst]	Rassist/in; rassistisch	
(to) **bully** sb. ['bʊli]	jn. tyrannisieren, mobben	verb: (to) **bully** – noun: **bully**
height [haɪt]	Höhe, (Körper-)Größe	Look at that tree! It must be at least 20 metres in ~. I'm the same ~ as my father now.
professional [prə'feʃənl]	professionell, Profi-	(F) professionnel, le (L) profiteri
peak [pi:k]	Gipfel, Spitze; Höhepunkt	The way up to the ~ is very steep. In 2010, the band were at the ~ of their success.
female ['fi:meɪl]	weiblich; weibliche Person; Weibchen	**Females** often earn less money than males. There are very few ~ workers at our factory.
male [meɪl]	männlich; männliche Person; Männchen	Most of the workers at our factory are ~. The police are looking for a 40-year-old ~. **male ◄► female**
the Olympic Games *(pl)* [əˌlɪmpɪk 'geɪmz] (*auch:* **the Olympics**)	die Olympischen Spiele	
(to) **admire** [əd'maɪə]	bewundern	She's a great artist. I ~ her paintings and sculptures. (F) admirer (L) admirari
league [li:g]	Liga	

(to) **empower** sb. [ɪm'paʊə]	jn. stärken; jn. befähigen/in die Lage versetzen *(, etwas zu tun)*	(to) give sb. the power to do sth. We like to ~ our workers to make their own decisions.
childhood ['tʃaɪldhʊd]	Kindheit	
(to) **criticize** sb. **(for)** ['krɪtɪsaɪz]	jn. kritisieren (wegen)	She was **~d for** her article in the school magazine. ! stress: **criticize** ['krɪtɪsaɪz] (F) critiquer
appearance [ə'pɪərəns]	Erscheinung(sbild), Aussehen	I was shocked by his ~ – he looked much older than the last time we met. verb: (to) **appear** – noun: **appearance** (F) l'apparence *(f)* (L) apparere
(to) **inspire** sb. [ɪn'spaɪə]	jn. inspirieren, jn. beflügeln, jn. anspornen	Frequent visits with his parents to the theatre **~d** him to attend drama school. (F) inspirer
outspoken [aʊt'spəʊkən]	direkt, geradeheraus, offen und ehrlich	She's very shy. Her sister is much more ~. You can hurt other people's feelings if you're too ~.
cultural ['kʌltʃərəl]	kulturell	noun: **culture** – adj: **cultural** ! stress: **culture, cultural** ['kʌltʃə], ['kʌltʃərəl] (F) culturel, le (L) colere *(pflegen, verehren)*
solidarity [ˌsɒlɪ'dærəti]	Solidarität	We'd like to express our ~ with the protesters.

recently ['riːsntli]	vor Kurzem, neulich; in letzter Zeit	I met my old class teacher in London ~. There have been a lot of accidents in our street ~. (F) récemment (L) recens (*frisch, neu*)
all-star team/player ['ɔːl stɑː]	Auswahlmannschaft/-spieler/in	
in a row [rəʊ]	in Folge, hintereinander, nacheinander	This has been the third dry summer **in a** ~.
record ['rekɔːd]	Rekord	Liam holds the ~ for the 100m at our school.
due to [djuː]	aufgrund, infolge	He had to give up his job ~ **to** bad health.
pandemic [pæn'demɪk]	Pandemie (*weltweite Epidemie*)	! stress: **pan<u>demic</u>** [pæn'demɪk]
successful [sək'sesfl]	erfolgreich	noun: **success** – verb: **successful**
passionate ['pæʃənət]	leidenschaftlich	She has a ~ interest in music. (F) passionné noun: **passion** ['pæʃn] (Passion, Leidenschaft) – adj: **passionate**
equal ['iːkwəl]	gleich	Do men and women really have ~ rights? (L) aequus, -a, -um (*gleich*)
minority [maɪ'nɒrəti]	Minderheit	There are 18 girls and 10 boys in my class. The boys are in the ~. (F) la minorité
indigenous [ɪn'dɪdʒənəs]	indigen, einheimisch; Ur-	Many ~ languages are in danger of dying out. The koala is ~ to Australia.

(to) **comment on** sth. ['kɒment]	etwas kommentieren, sich zu etwas äußern	When he saw his mum's new car, he just **~ed** "Nice!". The President didn't want to ~ **on** the news. (F) commenter
(to) **urge** sb. [ɜːdʒ]	jn. drängen; jn. eindringlich bitten	We **~d** other parents to teach their children to swim.
treatment ['triːtmənt]	Behandlung	He needed ~ on his leg after he fell off his horse. They protested against the ~ of indigenous Australians. (F) le traitement
individual [ˌɪndɪ'vɪdʒuəl]	Individuum, Einzelperson; einzelne(r, s), individuelle(r, s)	! stress: **individual** [ˌɪndɪ'vɪdʒuəl]
(to) **unlearn** sth. [ˌʌn'lɜːn]	etwas verlernen; etwas ablegen *(Angewohnheit)*	We can help you to ~ all your bad habits.
behaviour [bɪ'heɪvjə]	Verhalten; Benehmen	The twins' ~ had a bad effect on the whole class. verb: (to) **behave** – noun: **behaviour**
unless [ən'les]	es sei denn; außer (wenn)	You'll fail the test ~ you work harder. (= … if you don't work harder)
(to) **breathe** [briːð]	atmen	verb: (to) **breathe** [briːð] – noun: **breath** [breθ]
struggle ['strʌgl]	Ringen, Kampf	the **struggle** against racism/for peace = the fight against racism/for peace
(to) **care (about** sth.**)** [keə]	etwas ernst nehmen, etwas wichtig nehmen	She **~s** deeply **about** racism and discrimination. (L) carus, a, um (*lieb, teuer*)

court [kɔːt]	Spielfeld	 a basketball **court**  a tennis **court**
political [pəˈlɪtɪkl]	politisch	(F) politique
issue [ˈɪʃuː], [ˈɪsjuː]	Thema, (Streit-)Frage, Angelegenheit	Do you care about political **~s?**
p. 32 **sportsperson** [ˈspɔːtspɜːsn], **sportsman/sportswoman** *pl* **sportspeople** [ˈspɔːtspiːpl]	Sportler/in	
wetsuit [ˈwetsuːt]	Surfanzug, Taucheranzug	 a **wetsuit**

opal ['əʊpl]	Opal	 **opals**
influential [ˌɪnflu'enʃl]	einflussreich	noun: **influence** ['ɪnfluəns] (Einfluss) – adj: **influential**
silver ['sɪlvə]	Silber; silbern, Silber-	
medal ['medl]	Medaille	! stress: **<u>med</u>al** ['medl]

Unit 2 The Northeast of England

pp. 40/41 (to) **connect** [kə'nekt]	verbinden, verknüpfen	= (to) link
exhibition [ˌeksɪ'bɪʃn]	Ausstellung; Messe	Did you visit last month's technology ~? (F) l'exhibition (*f*) (L) exhibere (*vorführen*)
quayside ['kiːsaɪd]	Kai	We had a drink at one of the restaurants on/at the ~ and watched the boats.
angel ['eɪndʒl]	Engel	**angels** (F) l'ange (*m*) 

Part A

p. 42 **university** [ˌjuːnɪˈvɜːsəti]	Universität	(F) l'université (*f*) (L) universus
the library is more modern than it **used to be** [ˈjuːst tə]	die Bibliothek ist moderner als früher / als sie früher war	I **used to spend** a lot of time in the library when I was at university.
wise [waɪz]	weise	I don't think it's a ~ decision to leave school now.
lazy [ˈleɪzi]	faul	**hard-working** ◄► **lazy**

German "früher" – *used to* + infinitive / *would* + infinitive (► Grammar and practice 2.2, p. 144)

- With ***used to* + infinitive** we can talk about things that were true in the past but are not true any more:

We **used to live** in London.	Wir wohnten früher in London.
I **used to spend** lots of money on sweets.	Ich habe früher immer viel Geld für Süßigkeiten ausgegeben.

  Negative statements are made with ***didn't use to* …**, questions with ***Did* … *use to* …**:

He **didn't use to be** so shy.	Er war früher nicht so schüchtern.
Did you **use to cry** a lot when you were little?	Hast du (früher) viel geweint, als du klein warst?

- We use ***would* + infinitive (without *to*)** to talk about regular actions in the past:

Grandma **would take** us to the zoo every Sunday.	Oma ging (früher) jeden Sonntag mit uns in den Zoo. / Oma pflegte jeden Sonntag mit uns in den Zoo zu gehen.

residence [ˈrezɪdəns]	Wohnung, Wohnsitz	You should apply for a room in a students' ~. ! stress: **residence** [ˈrezɪdəns]

	certainly ['sɜːtnli]	sicher(lich), auf jeden Fall	This is a big problem, but we'll ~ solve it! adj: **certain** – adv: **certainly** (F) certainement (L) certus, -a, -um (*sicher*)
p. 43	**sarcasm** ['sɑːkæzəm]	Sarkasmus	! stress: **sarcasm** ['sɑːkæzəm]
	irony ['aɪrəni]	Ironie	! stress: **irony** ['aɪrəni]
	confusing [kən'fjuːzɪŋ]	verwirrend	The film was very **~**. I didn't understand what it was all about.
	non- [nɒn]	nicht-; Nicht-	· **non-** + adj: **non-British** (nicht-britisch) · **non-** + noun: **non-Brits** (Nicht-Briten)
p. 45	**playground** ['pleɪgraʊnd]	Spielplatz; Schulhof	a **playground** 
	educational [ˌedʒu'keɪʃənl]	lehrreich, informativ; Bildungs-	The presentation was very **~**. We learned a lot. There were children with different ~ backgrounds at the camp. noun: **education** – adj: **educational**

Part B

p. 48 (to) **receive** [rɪ'siːv]	erhalten, empfangen	a more formal word for (to) **get** (to) **receive a letter** ◄► (to) **send a letter** (F) recevoir (L) recipere
(to) **upload** sth. [ˌʌp'ləʊd]	etwas hochladen	
privacy ['prɪvəsi]	Privatsphäre	It's important to respect other people's ~. (L) privatus, a, um (*persönlich, nicht öffentlich*)
photographer [fə'tɒgrəfə]	Fotograf/in	· **photo(graph)** ['fəʊtəʊ, 'fəʊtəgrɑːf] Foto · (to) **photograph** ['fəʊtəgrɑːf] fotografieren · **photography** [fə'tɒgrəfi] Fotografie *(Hobby)* · **photographer** [fə'tɒgrəfə] Fotograf/in
status ['steɪtəs]	Status	Philip has just changed his ~ to "single". (L) status
(to) **unmute** [ˌʌn'mjuːt]	die Stummschaltung aufheben, deaktivieren	We can't hear you. You need to ~ your microphone.
microphone ['maɪkrəfəʊn]	Mikrofon	! pronunciation: **microphone** ['maɪkrəfəʊn]
(to) **overreact** [ˌəʊvəri'ækt]	überreagieren	= (to) react too strongly
sticker ['stɪkə]	Aufkleber	

	English	Deutsch	Example / Note
	(to) **be supposed to do** sth. [sə'pəʊzd]	etwas tun sollen	We**'re not ~ to** use our mobiles at school, but some of us do. I haven't heard their new album yet, but it**'s ~ to** be really good.
	conflict ['kɒnflɪkt]	Konflikt, Auseinandersetzung	! stress: **conflict** ['kɒnflɪkt] (F) le conflit
p. 49	**baddie** ['bædi] *(infml)*	Bösewicht, Schurke/Schurkin	I was the ~ in our last school play. I had to kill the king in the final act.
	wisdom ['wɪzdəm]	Weisheit	adj: **wise** [waɪz] – noun: **wisdom** ['wɪzdəm]
	(to) **troll** [trɒl], [trəʊl]	*sachlich falsche Dinge im Internet behaupten*	(to) write false messages on the internet
	(to) **identify** sb./sth. **(by** sth.**)** [aɪ'dentɪfaɪ]	jn./etwas identifizieren (anhand von etwas)	She **identified** the thief **by** his very big nose.
	original [ə'rɪdʒənl]	Original-, ursprüngliche(r, s)	! stress: **original** [ə'rɪdʒənl] (F) original, e (L) origo, inis f (*Ursprung*)
	you ought to … ['ɔːt tə]	du solltest …	Some people say we **~ to** stop eating meat. (= … we should stop eating meat.)
	(to) **chill** [tʃɪl] *(infml)*	sich entspannen, chillen; sich abregen	(to) relax

(to) **respect** sb./sth. (for) [rɪ'spekt]	jn./etwas respektieren, achten (wegen)	Our class teacher was always fair, and we **~ed** her **for** that. Ⓕ respecter verb: (to) **respect** – noun: **respect**
(to) **value** sth. ['vælju:]	etwas schätzen, wertschätzen; auf etwas Wert legen	Use a light when cycling at night if you ~ your life.
consent [kən'sent]	Einverständnis, Einwilligung	You'll need your parents' ~ to take part in the trip.
solution (to) [sə'lu:ʃn]	Lösung (für) *(Problem; Aufgabe)*	*English:* **the solution to** this problem *German:* **die Lösung für** dieses Problem / **die Lösung** dieses Problems Ⓕ la solution Ⓛ solvere (*lösen*)
personal ['pɜ:sənl]	persönlich	Could we meet? I need to talk about a ~ problem. Ⓕ personnel, le
friendship ['frendʃɪp]	Freundschaft	
safety ['seɪfti]	Sicherheit	adj: **safe** – noun: **safety**
request [rɪ'kwest]	Bitte, Wunsch	Nobody has reacted to my ~ for help. Ⓛ requirere
p. 51 (to) **shock** [ʃɒk]	schockieren	verb: (to) **shock** – adj: **shocked** – noun: **shock**
secret ['si:krət]	geheim	It was a ~ meeting. We didn't tell anyone about it. adj: **secret** – noun: **secret**

	English	German	Example
	indirectly [ˌɪndəˈrektli], [ˌɪndaɪˈrektli]	indirekt; auf indirekte Weise	**direct** *(adj)*; **directly** *(adv)* ◄► **indirect** *(adj)*; **indirectly** *(adv)*
p. 52	(to) **be attracted to** sb. [əˈtræktɪd]	sich zu jm. hingezogen fühlen	I'**m** really ~ **to** boys with blue eyes and a nice smile. (L) attrahere
	(to) **be seeing** sb.	mit jm. zusammen sein	They**'ve been** ~ each other for quite a while now, and next month they're getting married.
	(to) **fall in love (with** sb.**)**	sich (in jn.) verlieben	*English:* (to) **fall in love with sb.** *German:* **sich in jn. verlieben**
	(to) **date** sb. [deɪt]	mit jm. gehen, mit jm. zusammen sein	Dad **~d** Mum for years before they got married.
	(to) **break up (with** sb.**)** [ˌbreɪk‿ˈʌp]	Schluss machen (mit jm.), sich trennen (von jm.)	Jonathan's parents have **broken** ~ and are getting divorced soon.
	(to) **get to know** sb.	jn. kennenlernen	My parents **got to** ~ each other in high school.
	annoyed (with sb.**/ about** sth.**)** [əˈnɔɪd]	verärgert (über jn./etwas), irritiert	She was ~ **with** him because he was late again. My father often gets ~ **about** the government.
	confused [kənˈfjuːzd]	verwirrt	He looked so ~ – he clearly didn't understand you. ! **confused** = verwirrt – **confusing** = verwirrend (F) confus, e (L) confundere
	cross (with sb.**)** [krɒs]	böse, sauer (auf jn.)	Mum was ~ **with** me because I was late.
	frightened [ˈfraɪtnd]	verängstigt	Don't be ~. Thunder sounds scary but it isn't dangerous.

hopeful ['həʊpfl]	zuversichtlich, hoffnungsvoll	

hopeful – hopefully

- **hopeful** (*adj*) It might stop raining, but I'm not very **hopeful.**
- **hopefully** (*adv*) 1. We stood on the platform waiting **hopefully** for the train to arrive. (hoffnungsvoll, voller Hoffnung)
  2. **Hopefully** we'll have good weather for our picnic. (hoffentlich)

optimistic [ˌɒptɪ'mɪstɪk]	optimistisch	**optimistic** ◀▶ **pessimistic** [ˌpesɪ'mɪstɪk] Ⓕ optimiste ◀▶ pessimiste
pleased [pliːzd]	froh, erfreut, zufrieden	I'm really ~ with my new mobile. It's much better than my old one. *English:* **Pleased** to meet you. *German:* **Freut mich,** Sie kennenzulernen.
furious (with/at sb.**)** ['fjʊəriəs]	wütend, zornig (auf jn.), wutentbrannt	He was ~ when I told him. I've never seen anyone so angry. Ⓕ furieux, se Ⓛ furor m
heartbroken ['hɑːtbrəʊkən]	todunglücklich, untröstlich	Sally was ~ after her dog died.
terrified ['terɪfaɪd]	entsetzt	*English:* (to) **be terrified** (of sth.) Ⓕ terrifié, e *German:* **schreckliche Angst** (vor etwas) **haben**
thrilled [θrɪld]	begeistert	I was ~ when I was offered the leading role in the play.

	ex- [eks]	Ex-; ehemalige(r, s)	my **ex-**boyfriend/girlfriend; London's **ex-**mayor
	acquaintance [ə'kweɪntəns]	Bekannte(r)	I wouldn't say he's a real friend. He's just an **~.**
p. 53	**characterization** [ˌkærəktəraɪ'zeɪʃn]	Charakterisierung, Beschreibung	verb: (to) **characterize** ['kærəktəraɪz] (charakterisieren, beschreiben) noun: **characterization**
	gesture ['dʒestʃə]	Geste, Gebärde	The fans shouted and made rude **~s** at each other. It was a nice ~ to send me some chocolates.

Part C

p. 54	**matter** ['mætə]	Angelegenheit, Sache	We are here today to discuss the ~ of bullying.
	parenting ['peərəntɪŋ]	(Kindes-)Erziehung	
	psychologist [saɪ'kɒlədʒɪst]	Psychologe/Psychologin	! pronunciation and stress: **psychologist** [saɪ'kɒlədʒɪst]
	face-to-face [ˌfeɪs tə 'feɪs]	von Angesicht zu Angesicht	I don't like the telephone. I prefer talking **~-to-~.**
	average ['ævərɪdʒ]	durchschnittlich; Durchschnitt	The ~ age of students in our year is 16.5. I practise the piano two hours a day **on ~.** (= im Durchschnitt, durchschnittlich)
	length [leŋθ]	Länge; Dauer	The swimming pool has a ~ of 25 metres. I'd say the average ~ of films on DVD is 90 minutes. adj: **long** – noun: **length**

adolescent [ˌædəˈlesnt]	Heranwachsende(r), Jugendliche(r)	a young person about to become an adult
amount (of) [əˈmaʊnt]	Betrag, Menge; Höhe *(von Gehalt, Taschengeld)*	£ 300? I wouldn't pay that ~ for a pair of jeans. Now add a small ~ **of** salt to the soup.
percentage [pəˈsentɪdʒ]	Prozentsatz; prozentualer Anteil	What ~ of your pocket money do you spend on clothes? Ⓕ le pourcentage Ⓛ centum
(to) **trust** [trʌst]	trauen, vertrauen	She's a friend of mine. You can ~ her.
cyberbullying [ˈsaɪbəbʊliɪŋ]	Cyber-Mobbing *(Verleumdung o. Belästigung anderer im Internet)*	
communication [kəˌmjuːnɪˈkeɪʃn]	Kommunikation, Verständigung	Ⓕ la communication Ⓛ communis (*gemeinsam*)
role model [ˈrəʊl mɒdl]	Vorbild	Do you think your parents are a good **role** ~ for you?
p. 55 **pro** [prəʊ] (*kurz für:* **professional** [prəˈfeʃənl])	Profi-	At the age of 19 she became a ~ soccer player.
version [ˈvɜːʃn]	Version, Fassung	! stress: **version** [ˈvɜːʃn]

advertising *(no pl)* ['ædvətaɪzɪŋ]	Werbung; Werbe-	TV/online **advertising;** (to) work in **advertising;** **advertising** emails

advertising

· (to) **advertise** ['ædvətaɪz]	werben (für), Werbung machen (für); inserieren	*English:* (to) **advertise cars/furniture** *German:* **Werbung machen für Autos/Möbel**
· **advertising**	Werbung; Werbe-	The company spends millions on **advertising** each year.
· **advertisement** [əd'vɜːtɪsmənt] (*infml auch:* **ad** [æd], *BE auch:* **advert** ['ædvɜːt])	Werbung, Werbespot; Reklame; Anzeige, Inserat	You can find lots of job **advertisements** online. I always change channels during the **advertisements.** **banner ads = Bannerwerbung** (*im Internet*) **pop-up ads = Pop-up-Werbung** (*im Internet*)

p. 56	**billboard** ['bɪlbɔːd]	Plakatwand, Werbetafel	a large board with adverts at the side of the road or on a building
	commercial break [kəˌmɜːʃl 'breɪk]	Werbepause	the period of time when a TV film is stopped for adverts **commercial** = kommerziell, gewerblich
	influencer marketing ['ɪnfluənsə ˌmɑːkɪtɪŋ]	Multiplikatoren-Marketing *(der Einsatz von Social-Media-Meinungsführer/innen zu Werbezwecken)*	a form of social media marketing that uses endorsements and product placement from influencers

	product placement [ˌprɒdʌkt ˈpleɪsmənt]	Produktplatzierung *(Schleichwerbung)*	the use of certain products in films or television programmes as a form of advertising
	file [faɪl]	Datei, File	(to) open/close/copy/save/email a **file**
	according to [əˈkɔːdɪŋ tə]	laut, zufolge	**According ~** the papers, they have left the country. But I'm not so sure.
p. 57	**bar chart** [ˈbɑː tʃɑːt]	Balkendiagramm	
	pie chart [ˈpaɪ tʃɑːt]	Tortendiagramm	
	chart [tʃɑːt]	Tabelle, Schaubild	

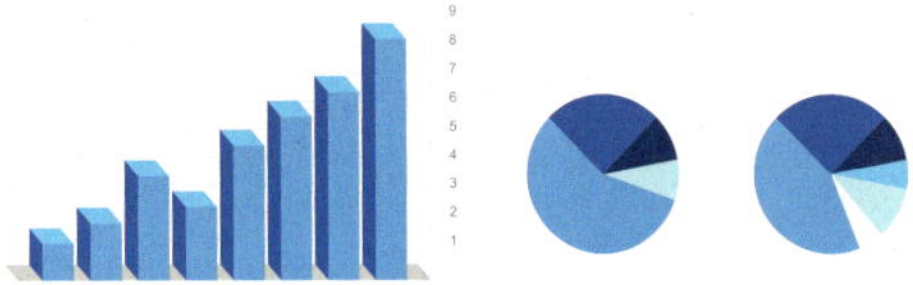

a **bar chart** — **pie charts**

	daily [ˈdeɪli]	täglich	noun: **day** – adj/adv: **daily**
	(to) **socialize** [ˈsəʊʃəlaɪz]	sich treffen, Kontakt pflegen	(to) meet people, (to) spend time with people
	gender [ˈdʒendə]	(soziales) Geschlecht, Gender	There are ~ differences, of course, but men and women should still be equal. Ⓛ genus, eris n (*Geschlecht*)
p. 58	(to) **insist on** sth. [ɪnˈsɪst]	auf etwas bestehen	I didn't want to go to the Millers but Mum **~ed.** Dad always **~s on** me helping him clean the car. Ⓕ insister Ⓛ insistere
	household [ˈhaʊshəʊld]	Haushalt; Haushalts-	

chore [tʃɔː]	(Haus-)Arbeit; *(lästige)* Pflicht	What **~s** do you do at home? – I wash the dishes and walk the dog.
in return [ɪn rɪ'tɜːn]	als Gegenleistung	I gave her some flowers **in ~** for her help.
value ['væljuː]	Wert	Do young people share older people's **~s?** The ~ of our car has gone down by £ 2000 since I bought it. (F) la valeur (L) valere verb: (to) **value** – noun: **value**
(to) **budget** ['bʌdʒɪt]	haushalten	My grandparents didn't have much money when they were young. They had to ~ carefully. verb: (to) **budget** – noun: **budget** (Budget)
tricky ['trɪki]	heikel, verzwickt, knifflig	a **tricky** situation/problem/question/business
very *(adj)*	genau	We talked about this ~ subject at school last week. (… über genau dieses Thema …)
regardless (of) [rɪ'gɑːdləs]	ungeachtet	We spent a lot of time outside ~ of the bad weather.
cash flow ['kæʃ fləʊ]	Cashflow *(die finanzielle Situation)*	**cash** = Bargeld; *(infml auch:)* Geld *English:* (to) **pay cash** – *German:* **bar bezahlen**
vital ['vaɪtl]	unerlässlich; unverzichtbar; (lebens)wichtig	Regular meals are ~ for your dog's health.
expense	Ausgabe	the money you spend on sth.
(to) **override**	aufheben, außer Kraft setzen	

They **run out of** money.	Ihnen geht das Geld aus. / Bei ihnen wird das Geld knapp.	

> **(to) run out (knapp werden; zu Ende gehen)**
>
> - **Time is running out.** — Die Zeit wird knapp.
> - **We're running out of time.** — Wir haben keine Zeit mehr.
> - **It was so hot that the shops ran out of cold drinks.** — …, dass den Geschäften die kalten Getränke ausgingen.

	(to) **balance** sth. **out** [ˌbæləns'aʊt]	etwas ausbalancieren, etwas ins Gleichgewicht bringen	
	(to) **encourage** sb. [ɪn'kʌrɪdʒ]	jn. ermutigen, jn. ermuntern	My parents **~d** me to go abroad for a year.
	perhaps [pə'hæps]	vielleicht	= maybe
	piggy bank ['pɪgi bæŋk]	Sparschwein	
	account [ə'kaʊnt]	Konto, Account	You'll need your ID card to open a bank **~**. How do I change the password of my email ~ ?
	(to) **accumulate** sth. [ə'kju:mjəleɪt]	etwas ansammeln	Every family **~s** quite a lot of things over the years: clothes, books, furniture, toys, …
p. 59	**agreement** [ə'gri:mənt]	Einigung; Vereinbarung	After a long discussion, we finally reached **~.** (… haben wir uns schließlich geeinigt.)

	(to) **express** [ɪk'spres]	ausdrücken, zum Ausdruck bringen	"In my opinion", "In my view" and "I think" are good phrases to ~ your opinion. (L) exprimere
	Go ahead. [ˌɡəʊ‿ə'hed]	Leg los. / Fang an. / Nur zu.	"Let me explain, please." – "OK, **go** ~ then."
	(to) **concentrate (on** sth.**)** ['kɒnsntreɪt]	sich konzentrieren (auf etwas)	Please be quiet. I can't ~ **on** my work. ! stress: **concentrate** ['kɒnsntreɪt] (F) concentrer
	(to) **agree to disagree** (*auch:* (to) **agree to differ)**	sich darauf einigen, dass man verschiedener Ansicht ist; einsehen, dass man sich nicht einigen kann	The argument could have gone on and on, so we **~d to disagree.**

Access to cultures: Talking about problems

p. 66	**fault** [fɔːlt]	Schuld, Fehler	Why didn't you wake me up? It's your ~ that I'll be late for school.
p. 67	**lie** [laɪ]	Lüge	He says I took the money, but that's a ~. (to) **tell lies** = lügen (to) **tell sb. lies** = jn. anlügen, jn. belügen
	(to) **mishear** sb. [ˌmɪs'hɪə], **misheard, misheard** [ˌmɪs'hɜːd]	jn. falsch verstehen	You must have **~d** him. I'm sure he didn't say that.

(to) **blame** sb. **(for** sth.**)** [bleɪm]	jm. die Schuld geben (an etwas); jm. Vorwürfe machen (wegen etwas)	She **~d** her husband **for** their son's death. Don't ~ me. It wasn't my fault.
method ['meθəd]	Methode	the way of doing something ! stress: **method** ['meθəd]

Unit 3 The Southwest of the USA

Part A

p. 70	**road trip** ['rəʊd trɪp] *(bes. AE)*	Autoreise, *(lange)* Autofahrt	I'd like to go on a **road** ~ across the USA.
	(to) **hand** sth. **down** [ˌhænd 'daʊn]	weitergeben; vererben	(to) give sth. to sb. who is younger than you They try to ~ **down** the skills to the next generation.
	security scanner [sɪ'kjʊərəti skænə]	Sicherheitsscanner	At nearly all airports you have to go through a **security ~.**
	recess ['riːses] *(AE)*	Pause *(zwischen Schulstunden)*	= *BE* **break**

transport ['trænspɔːt]	Transport(wesen); Verkehrsmittel	stress: **transport** ['trænspɔːt] (F) le transport (L) trans + portare different forms of **transport**  **public transport** *(BE)* / **public transportation** *(AE)* = öffentliche Verkehrsmittel
company ['kʌmpəni]	Firma	My uncle works for an oil ~ in Scotland.
part-time	Teilzeit-, Halbtags-	**part-time** ◄► **full-time** (Vollzeit-, Ganztags-) ! stress: **a part-time job** [ˌpɑːt taɪm 'dʒɒb] / **a full-time job** [ˌfʊl taɪm 'dʒɒb] (to) **work part-time** [ˌpɑːt 'taɪm] / (to) **work full-time** [ˌfʊl 'taɪm]
allowance [ə'laʊəns] *(bes. AE)*	Taschengeld	= *BE* **pocket money**
petrol ['petrəl] *(BE)* **/** **gas** [gæs] *(AE)*	Benzin	a **petrol station** *(BE)* / **gas station** *(AE)* 
sophomore ['sɒfəmɔː] *(AE)*	*Schüler/in in der 10. Klasse der High School;* *Student/in im zweiten Studienjahr*	

p. 71	(to) **run** a school / a company / a hotel/…, **ran, run**	eine Schule / eine Firma / ein Hotel/… leiten, führen	My uncle **~s** a motel near New Orleans.
	ability [ə'bɪlɪti]	Fähigkeit, Können	Joanna shows great scientific **~.** adj: **able** – noun: **ability**
	(to) **vary** ['veəri]	variieren, schwanken	House prices ~ a lot, depending on the region.
	academic [ˌækə'demɪk]	wissenschaftlich, akademisch	**academic credits** *(pl)* = Anrechnungspunkte (für das Studium); Leistungsnachweis
	range [reɪndʒ]	Bereich, Bandbreite, Palette	The new language school offers a wide ~ of courses.
	junior year ['dʒuːniə jɪə]	*10. Klasse der High School*	
	senior year ['siːniə jɪə]	Abschlussklasse, -jahr	
	in order to do sth. ['ɔːdə]	um etwas zu tun	We have to win this match **in ~ to** qualify for the finals.
	(to) **develop** [dɪ'veləp]	entwickeln, weiterentwickeln; sich entwickeln	Our company **~s** and sells software. (F) développer The village **~ed** into a town in only ten years.
	smart [smɑːt] *(bes. BE)*	elegant, schick; gepflegt	He looked really ~ in his new suit. She likes to wear ~ clothes.
	assessment [ə'sesmənt]	Beurteilung, Bewertung	noun: **assessment** – verb: (to) **assess** (beurteilen, bewerten)

High School Diploma	*Schulabschluss in den USA (mit Hochschulzugangsberechtigung)*	
secondary school ['sekəndri skuːl]	weiterführende Schule *(in GB)*	· **primary school** = a school for children between the ages of 4 or 5 and 11 · **secondary school** = a school for young people between the ages of 11 and 16 or 18
comprehensive school [ˌkɒmprɪ'hensɪv skuːl]	*einer deutschen Gesamtschule vergleichbare Schulform in GB*	
grammar school ['græmə skuːl]	*einem deutschen Gymnasium vergleichbare Schulform in GB*	
academy [ə'kædəmi]	Akademie, (Fach-)Hochschule; *(in GB:) unabhängige, direkt von der Regierung finanzierte Schule*	
(to) **fund** [fʌnd]	finanzieren	(to) **fund** a project / a museum / a festival / … a publicly/privately **funded** organization
curriculum [kə'rɪkjələm], *pl* **curriculums** *or* **curricula** [kə'rɪkjələ]	Lehrplan	the subjects which are taught at each type of school; the content which is taught in each subject (L) curriculum (*Verlauf*)

	GCSE [ˌdʒiː siː‿es 'iː] **(= General Certificate of Secondary Education** [ˌdʒenrəl sətɪfɪkət‿əv ˌsekəndri‿edʒu'keɪʃn]**)**	*Prüfung für Schüler/innen ab 15, mittlerer Schulabschluss*	a set of exams which British students take at school when they're around 15 or 16
	(to) **focus on** ['fəʊkəs]	fokussieren auf, abzielen auf	Our language courses ~ **on** improving the students' communication skills.
	A level ['eɪ levl] (= **advanced level** [əd'vɑːnst levl]**)**	*Prüfungen zur Hochschulzulassungsberechtigung (etwa wie Abitur)*	
	advanced [əd'vɑːnst]	fortgeschritten; für Fortgeschrittene	Are you attending the beginners' or the ~ course? (F) avancé, e
p. 72	**civil war** [ˌsɪvl 'wɔː]	Bürgerkrieg	(F) civil (L) civis m, f (*Bürger/in*)
	one third [θɜːd]	ein Drittel	1/2 = a/one **half** (*pl.* **halves**) 1/3 = a/one **third** 1/4 = a/one **quarter;** a/one **fourth** *(AE)* 1/5 = a/one **fifth** 1/6 = a/one **sixth**
	atom bomb ['ætəm bɒm]	Atombombe	
	(to) **launch** [lɔːntʃ]	starten, einleiten, einführen, auf den Markt bringen	(to) **launch** a business / a programme / a project (to) **launch** an attack; (to) **launch** a space ship

	reception [rɪ'sepʃn]	Empfang *(Hotel u.Ä.)*	**receptionist** [rɪ'sepʃənɪst] = Empfangschef/in
	stay [steɪ]	Aufenthalt	verb: (to) **stay** – noun: **stay**
p. 73	(to) **swing** [swɪŋ], **swung, swung** [swʌŋ]	schwingen	The sofa was so high that she could ~ her legs.
	bat [bæt]	Schläger, Schlagholz *(Baseball, Kricket, Tischtennis)*	**swinging a baseball bat** 
p. 74	**loyal** ['lɔɪəl]	loyal	! stress: **loyal** ['lɔɪəl] (F) loyal, e
	ambitious [æm'bɪʃəs]	ehrgeizig	adj: **ambitious** – (L) ambitiosus, -a, -um noun: **ambition** (Ehrgeiz, Bestreben)
	bossy ['bɒsi]	herrisch, rechthaberisch	adj: **bossy** – noun: **boss**
	cautious ['kɔːʃəs]	vorsichtig	= careful (L) cautus, -a, -um adj: **cautious** – noun: **caution** (Vorsicht)
	enthusiastic (about) [ɪn,θjuːzi'æstɪk]	begeistert (von)	Jack is ~ **about** cooking. His meals are delicious.
	generous ['dʒenərəs]	großzügig	adj: **generous** – noun: **generosity** [,dʒenə'rɒsəti] (Großzügigkeit) (F) généreux/-se (L) generosus, -a, -um

hard-working [ˌhɑːd ˈwɜːkɪŋ]	fleißig	**hard-working** people = people who work hard
mean [miːn]	gemein, fies; geizig	I hate my brother. He's often really ~ to me. Joe won't buy you a drink. He's very ~ with money. adj: **mean** – noun: **meanness**
reliable [rɪˈlaɪəbl]	verlässlich, zuverlässig	She's a very ~ person. If she says she'll help you, then she'll do it. adj: **reliable** – noun: **reliability** [rɪˌlaɪəˈbɪləti]
tolerant (of) [ˈtɒlərənt]	tolerant (gegenüber)	I'm very ~ **of** others even if I don't agree with them. adj: **tolerant** – noun: **tolerance** stress: **<u>to</u>lerant, <u>to</u>lerance** [ˈtɒlərənt], [ˈtɒlərəns] (F) tolérant, e (L) tolerare (ertragen)
jealousy [ˈdʒeləsi]	Eifersucht	adj: **jealous** – noun: **jealousy** (F) la jalousie
responsibility [rɪˌspɒnsəˈbɪləti]	Verantwortung	Having children is a big ~. (F) la responsabilité adj: **responsible** [rɪˈspɒnsəbl] – noun: **responsibility** [rɪˌspɒnsəˈbɪləti]

Prefixes expressing the opposite

dis-

advantage – **dis**advantage
(to) appear – (to) **dis**appear
honest – **dis**honest
honesty – **dis**honesty
(to) like – (to) **dis**like
respectful – **dis**respectful

in-

correct – **in**correct
formal – **in**formal
tolerant – **in**tolerant

im- (*before* **p** and **b**)

patience – **im**patience
patient – **im**patient
polite – **im**polite
possible – **im**possible
practical – **im**practical

ir- (*before* **r**)

regular – **ir**regular
responsible – **ir**responsible

un-

friendly – **un**friendly
happy – **un**happy
healthy – **un**healthy
kind – **un**kind
reliable – **un**reliable
usual – **un**usual

p. 75	**documentary** [ˌdɒkju'mentri]	Dokumentarfilm	stress: **docu<u>men</u>tary** [ˌdɒkju'mentri]
	narration [nə'reɪʃn]	Erzählung, Schilderung	(F) la narration
	host [həʊst]	Gastgeber/in; Moderator/in	

Part B

p. 78	(to) **be hard on** sb. [hɑːd]	streng mit jm. sein; hart mit jm. umgehen	Don't **be** so ~ **on** your brother. He's only 5 years old.
	cashier [kæ'ʃɪə]	Kassierer/in	a person who works at a cash desk

bulletin board ['bʊlətɪn bɔːd] (*BE auch:* **noticeboard)**	Schwarzes Brett *(auch elektronisch)*	Please look at our ~ **board** for further details.
résumé [*BE:* 'rezjuːmeɪ, *AE:* 'rezəmeɪ] *(AE)*	Lebenslauf	
CV (curriculum vitae) [ˌsiː 'vi, kəˌrɪkjələm 'viːtaɪ] *(BE)*	Lebenslauf	At the age of 15, your ~ is probably not very long.
(to) **serve** [sɜːv]	servieren; bedienen	Breakfast will be **~d** at 8 o'clock. We had to wait ages until someone came to ~ us.
customer ['kʌstəmə]	Kunde/Kundin	Serving **~s** all evening can be quite stressful.
(to) **volunteer**	ehrenamtliche Arbeit leisten; sich freiwillig melden, sich bereit erklären	There are lots of ways to ~ in your community. Hundreds of doctors **~ed** to help after the flood. noun: **volunteer** – verb: (to) **volunteer** **volunteer work** = ehrenamtliche Arbeit
though *(adv)* [ðəʊ]	allerdings; trotzdem	! **though** = **1.** *(conj)* We kept working in the garden **though** it was raining. (**obwohl**) **2.** *(adv)* Nice day, isn't it? – Yes, it is. A bit cold, **though. (allerdings)** She can be quite rude sometimes. I like her a lot, **though. (trotzdem)**

Access to cultures: Student jobs in the USA

p. 79	(to) **suffer (from)** ['sʌfə]	leiden (an, unter)	I don't like to see animals ~**ing.** I sometimes ~ **from** bad headaches.
	labour ['leɪbə] (*AE:* **labor)**	Arbeit	work, especially physical work
	federal ['fedərəl]	Bundes-, bundesstaatlich	Germany is a ~ **republic.** (Bundesrepublik)
	minor ['maɪnə]	Minderjährige(r)	a person who is not yet an adult
	exception [ɪk'sepʃn]	Ausnahme	Most families in our street have two cars, but the Millers are an ~ – they only have one.
	such as ['sʌtʃ‿əz]	wie etwa	ball sports **such** ~ football, basketball or hockey (= ball sports **like** football, basketball or hockey)
	(to) **deliver** [dɪ'lɪvə]	liefern, ausliefern	Hungry? We ~ pizzas to your door.
	(to) **employ** sb. [ɪm'plɔɪ]	jn. anstellen, jn. beschäftigen	to give sb. a paid job

(to) employ – employer – employee – …

• (to) **employ sb.**	jn. anstellen, beschäftigen	In the summer we **employ** lots of students. The company **employs** over 1,000 people.
• **employer** [ɪm'plɔɪə]	Arbeitgeber/in	The company is the biggest **employer** in this area.
• **employee** [ɪm'plɔɪiː]	Arbeitnehmer/in	The company has over 1,000 **employees.**
• **employment** [ɪm'plɔɪmənt]	Anstellung, Arbeit	Lots of people are looking for **employment.**
• **unemployment** [ˌʌnɪm'plɔɪmənt]	Arbeitslosigkeit	**Unemployment** is a huge problem where we live.
• **unemployed** [ˌʌnɪm'plɔɪd]	arbeitslos	Dad was **unemployed** for a year. Now he has a new job.
• **self-employed** [ˌself‿ɪm'plɔɪd]	selbstständig	My aunt is a **self-employed** architect.

harvest ['hɑːvɪst]	Ernte	
aged [eɪdʒd]	im Alter von	We're looking for volunteers ~ between 18 and 30.
…-based [beɪst]	…-basiert	We offer **cloud-based** / **internet-based** / **web-based** solutions for your business. My sister works for a **London-based** company. (… in London ansässige Firma.)
(to) **influence** ['ɪnfluəns]	beeinflussen	Even today, the Beatles still ~ musicians all over the world. An **influencer** is a person who recommends certain products or services on social media.

	internship ['ɪntɜːnʃɪp]	Praktikum	I did an ~ at a small marketing company.
	minimum wage [ˌmɪnɪməm 'weɪdʒ]	Mindestlohn	the lowest wage that an employer is allowed to pay **minimum** (Minimum) ◄► **maximum** ['mæksɪməm] (Maximum)
	low [ləʊ]	niedrig	**low** ◄► **high**
	rate [reɪt]	Rate, Quote	a high success ~ / unemployment ~ / death ~ Do you have a **flat** ~ for your phone? (Flatrate, Pauschalpreis)
	organization [ˌɔːgənaɪ'zeɪʃn] (*BE auch:* **organisation)**	Organisation	! stress: **organization** [ˌɔːgənaɪ'zeɪʃn] verb: (to) **organize** – noun: **organization** (F) l'organisation *(f)*
p. 80	**purpose** ['pɜːpəs]	Absicht, Sinn, Zweck, Ziel	**on purpose** = mit Absicht, absichtlich I think Dad lost our last chess match **on purpose.**
	intention [ɪn'tenʃn]	Absicht, Vorsatz	what you plan to do (F) l'intention *(f)* I have no ~ of attending the meeting.
	case [keɪs]	Fall	**In case of** fire do not use elevator!  (L) casus, us m You should take an umbrella **in case** it rains. (... falls es regnet ...)

(to) **ignore** [ɪɡ'nɔː]	nicht beachten, ignorieren	They **~d** all the warning signs. (F) ignorer (L) ignorare (*nicht wissen*)
attention [ə'tenʃn]	Aufmerksamkeit	(F) l'attention (*f*) (L) attentus, a, um (*aufmerksam*)

attention

(to) **attract/catch/grab sb.'s attention**	It was his smile that first **attracted my attention.** He shouted to **grab/catch her attention.**	jemandes Aufmerksamkeit erregen; jemandes Aufmerksamkeit gewinnen
(to) **draw attention to sth.**	How can we **draw attention to** those problems? May **I draw your attention to** a few mistakes?	auf etwas aufmerksam machen; die Aufmerksamkeit auf etwas lenken
(to) **pay attention (to)**	Stop talking now and **pay attention.** You never **pay attention** to what I'm saying.	aufmerksam sein, aufpassen; zuhören, Beachtung schenken

attractive [ə'træktɪv]	attraktiv, verlockend	I like this idea – it's very ~. (L) attrahere (*anziehen*) verb: (to) **attract** – noun: **attraction** – adj: **attractive**
effort ['efət]	Anstrengung; Bemühung, Mühe	! (to) **make an effort** = **1.** sich Mühe geben; **2.** Anstrengungen unternehmen

Part C

p. 82	**guideline** ['gaɪdlaɪn]	Richtlinie, Richtschnur	
	strength [streŋθ]	Stärke, Kraft	adjectives: **strong** ◄► **weak** nouns: **strength** ◄► **weakness**
	recent ['riːsnt]	aktuell, neu; kürzlich geschehen/erfolgt	(F) récent, récemment (L) recens

recent, recently

recent (*adj*)	The band's **most recent** CD was their most successful.	neueste, jüngste
	Make a list of all your holiday jobs. Start with the **most recent.**	aktuellsten
	I've started doing more sport **in recent months.**	in den letzten Monaten
	A **recent discovery** shows that …	eine kürzlich gemachte Entdeckung
recently (*adv*)	I met my ex-boyfriend **recently.**	vor Kurzem, neulich, kürzlich
	Their **recently published** book was a huge success.	kürzlich veröffentlicht
	There have been a lot of accidents in our street **recently.**	in letzter Zeit

(to) **increase** [ɪn'kriːs]	erhöhen, steigern, vergrößern; (an)steigen, zunehmen	They have **~d** the price of the book to €20. House prices in London have **~d** again. (L) increscere (*anwachsen*)
qualification [ˌkwɒlɪfɪ'keɪʃn]	Qualifikation	What **~s** do you need for this job? (F) la qualification
(to) **achieve** [ə'tʃiːv]	erreichen *(Ziel)*, erzielen *(Resultat)*; zustande bringen	Hmm, this isn't the result we wanted to **~**. I've been working all day, but I haven't **~d** much.

fellow *(vor Nomen)* ['feləʊ]	Mit-	**fellow students** = Mitstudierende **fellow team mates** = Teamkolleg/innen **fellow Americans** = amerikanische Landsleute
outstanding [aʊt'stændɪŋ]	hervorragend, außergewöhnlich	an **outstanding** singer/result/success
certificate [sə'tɪfɪkət]	Urkunde, Bescheinigung; Zeugnis	! stress: **certificate** [sə'tɪfɪkət]
sustainability [səˌsteɪnə'bɪləti]	Nachhaltigkeit, Zukunftsfähigkeit	adj: **sustainable** [sə'steɪnəbl] (nachhaltig, umweltverträglich; zukunftsfähig) – noun: **sustainability**
prestigious [pre'stɪdʒəs]	angesehen, renommiert, prestigeträchtig	a **prestigious** award/school/competition
scientific [ˌsaɪən'tɪfɪk]	(natur)wissenschaftlich	noun: **science** – adj: **scientific** (F) scientifique (L) scientia (*Wissen*)
researcher [rɪ'sɜːtʃə], ['riːsɜːtʃə]	Forscher/in	
knowledge *(no pl)* ['nɒlɪdʒ]	Wissen; Kenntnis(se)	Matt has a great ~ of Latin and Greek. verb: (to) **know** [nəʊ] – noun: **knowledge** ['nɒlɪdʒ]
duty ['djuːti]	Aufgabe, Pflicht	(to) **be on duty** = im Dienst sein, Dienst haben (to) **be off duty** = außer Dienst sein, keinen Dienst haben

(to) **involve** [ɪn'vɒlv]	bestehen aus, beinhalten, mit sich bringen; einbeziehen, beteiligen	Charity projects often ~ a lot of work. Your tasks will ~ serving customers and washing up. It's important to ~ everybody in the decision.
(to) **assist (with)** [ə'sɪst]	assistieren, helfen (bei)	Could you ~ me **with** my report? **How may we ~?** (*im Geschäft:* Wie können wir Ihnen helfen/behilflich sein?) Ⓕ assister Ⓛ assistere (*beistehen*)
elderly ['eldəli]	ältere(r, s)	an **elderly** couple; **elderly** residents **the elderly** *(pl)* = ältere Menschen
member ['membə]	Mitglied	**Nur für Mitglieder!**  Ⓕ le membre
p. 83 **applicant** ['æplɪkənt]	Bewerber/in	There were over 30 **~s** for the job. Ⓛ applicare verb: (to) **apply** – nouns: **application** [ˌæplɪ'keɪʃn] (Bewerbung); *(person)* **applicant**
courteous ['kɜːtiəs]	höflich	polite, showing respect
outdoors [ˌaʊt'dɔːz]	im Freien, draußen	adj: **outdoor** – **outdoor** activities/sports adv: **outdoors** – I like to be **outdoors.**

definite ['defɪnət]	bestimmte(r, s); definitiv, endgültig, eindeutig	Have you got any ~ plans for the weekend? I need a ~ answer by tomorrow. adj: **definite** – adv: **definitely** (sicher, bestimmt)
plus [plʌs] *(infml)*	Plus, Vorteil	an advantage Good computer skills are a definite **~.**
(to) **hold** [həʊld], **held, held** [held]	abhalten *(Veranstaltung)*	(to) **hold** a meeting/a competition/an interview
in person [ɪn 'pɜːsn]	persönlich	Interviews can be held online or **in ~.**
laboratory [lə'bɒrətri] (*infml:* **lab** [læb])	Labor	working in a science **lab** 
(to) **provide** [prə'vaɪd]	(an)bieten, zur Verfügung stellen	• We can't ~ equipment for so many people. • (to) **provide sb. with sth.** = jn. mit etwas versorgen, jm. etwas zur Verfügung stellen – We can't ~ so many people **with** equipment. (L) providere (*vorsorgen*)
(to) **gain** [geɪn]	bekommen; gewinnen	= (to) get; (to) win (to) **gain** confidence/experience/strength/...

variety [vəˈraɪəti]	Vielzahl, Auswahl	Germany is known for the ~ of its bread. (F) la variété (L) varietas, atis *f* (*Verschiedenheit*)
engineering [ˌendʒɪˈnɪərɪŋ]	Ingenieurwesen, Maschinenbau	She studied ~ and became an engineer.
(to) **consist of** [kənˈsɪst]	bestehen aus	My family **~s of** my parents, my two sisters and me.
participant (in) [pɑːˈtɪsɪpənt]	Teilnehmer/in (an)	The **participants in** the competition were not allowed to talk to each other. verb: (to) **participate (in)** [pɑːˈtɪsɪpeɪt] *(fml)* (teilnehmen (an), sich beteiligen (an)) – noun *(person)*: **participant (in)**
competitive [kəmˈpetətɪv]	leistungsorientiert, ehrgeizig; wettbewerbsorientiert	Olivia is very ~ and always wants to win. This isn't a ~ race – it's just for fun. noun: **competition** – adj: **competitive**
motivated [ˈməʊtɪveɪtɪd]	motiviert	a **motivated** applicant/student (F) motivé, e
(to) **meet** [miːt], **met, met** [met]	einhalten, erfüllen *(Kriterien, Bedingungen, Anforderungen)*	I didn't get the job because I didn't ~ the conditions. (…, weil ich die Bedingungen nicht erfüllte) ! (to) **meet** = **1.** (sich) treffen; kennenlernen **2.** einhalten, erfüllen
requirement [rɪˈkwaɪəmənt] (*meist pl*: **requirements)**	Voraussetzung, Anforderung	We offer web-based solutions that meet all your **~s.**
(to) **maintain** [meɪnˈteɪn]	beibehalten, aufrecht erhalten; instand halten, unterhalten	We always try everything to ~ our high standards. A castle is very expensive to **~.** (L) manu tenere (*in der Hand halten*)

	document ['dɒkjumənt]	Dokument	! stress: **document** ['dɒkjumənt] (F) le document
	letter of reference ['refrəns]	Empfehlungsschreiben, Referenz(schreiben)	You can ask your teacher to write a **letter of ~** for your application.
p. 84	**Dear Sir or Madam, …** *(BE)* [sɜː], ['mædəm]	Sehr geehrte Damen und Herren, …	! When you write a formal letter to a person whose name you don't know, you start your letter with **Dear Sir or Madam.**
	pleasure ['pleʒə]	Vergnügen	*English:* **It is my pleasure** to introduce to you our guest tonight. *German:* **Es ist mir ein Vergnügen,** Ihnen unseren heutigen Gast vorzustellen.
	personality [ˌpɜːsə'næləti]	Persönlichkeit	all aspects of a person's character (F) la personnalité
	peer [pɪə]	*Angehörige(r) derselben Alters- oder Berufsgruppe*	She didn't want to fail in front of all her **~s** / in front of her **~ group.**
	(to) **demonstrate** sth. ['demənstreɪt]	etwas zeigen, demonstrieren, nachweisen	! • (to) **demonstrate** sth. = etwas zeigen, nachweisen, unter Beweis stellen • (to) **demonstrate for/against** sth. = für/gegen etwas demonstrieren
	(to) **prove** [pruːv]	nachweisen, beweisen	Is that right? Can you ~ it? (F) prouver (L) probare

(to) **handle** sth. ['hændl]	etwas handhaben, mit etwas umgehen (können), mit etwas fertig werden	It'll be interesting to see how they ~ the situation. The new job is quite challenging. I just hope I can ~ the responsibility.
highly ['haɪli]	sehr, höchst, äußerst, ausgesprochen	I can ~ recommend this film. It's a ~ interesting/surprising/successful film.

Intensifying adverbs [ɪn'tensɪfaɪɪŋ] **(Verstärkende Adverbien)**

absolutely right	völlig richtig	**highly** motivated	höchst motiviert
completely normal	völlig normal, ganz normal	**terribly** tired	schrecklich müde
especially helpful	besonders hilfreich	**totally** wrong	völlig falsch
extremely hot	äußerst heiß	**very** confused	sehr verwirrt

	(to) **hesitate** ['hezɪteɪt]	zögern	Don't ~ to get in touch if there is anything I can do. (F) hésiter
	Yours sincerely [ˌjɔːz sɪn'sɪəli] *(BE)*	Mit freundlichen Grüßen *(Briefschluss)*	
p. 85	(to) **advertise** ['ædvətaɪz]	Werbung machen (für); inserieren	*English:* (to) **advertise** clothes/cars/… *German:* **für** Kleidung/Autos/… **werben** verb: (to) **advertise** ['ædvətaɪz] – noun: **advertisement** [əd'vɜːtɪsmənt] (*kurz auch:* **ad** [æd], **advert** ['ædvɜːt])
	ideal [aɪ'dɪəl]	ideal	! stress: **ideal** [aɪ'dɪəl] (F) idéal

(to) **consider** [kən'sɪdə]	erwägen, in Betracht/in Erwägung ziehen; berücksichtigen	They **~ed** moving to the country but in the end decided against it. (F) considérer (L) considerare (*überlegen*)

(to) **consider**

1. erwägen, in Betracht/in Erwägung ziehen; berücksichtigen	Thank you for your letter. We will **consider** your ideas and suggestions for improvement. Are you **considering** attending one of our courses? Send us an email. I hope the company will **consider** my application.
2. nachdenken über; bedenken, abwägen	Now is the time to **consider** your position. The answer to that request should be **considered** very carefully. Before you start, **consider** the following questions: … I think unemployment is a big problem, especially **considering** how many young people are out of work. (… besonders, wenn man bedenkt/berücksichtigt, …)
3. betrachten als, halten für	The Rolling Stones **are considered (to be)** one of the greatest rock bands in the world. Agree on three points that you **consider (to be)** important.

Greetings, … *(pl)* ['griːtɪŋz]	Grüße	Warm **greetings** to you all!
p. 86 **occasion** [ə'keɪʒn]	Gelegenheit; Ereignis, Anlass	We only go to restaurants on certain **~s.** (F) l'occasion (*f*) (L) occasio
(to) **hire** ['haɪə]	*(Person)* einstellen; mieten, leihen	We need to ~ three more people for the project. They **~d** a car and drove to the coast.

Text Good behaviour in the workplace

p. 87	(to) **promote** [prəˈməʊt]	fördern	Keeping active **~s** good health. (to) **promote** products/a new book (bewerben, Werbung machen für) (to) **promote** sb. (jn. befördern)
	(to) **deserve** [dɪˈzɜːv]	verdienen *(zu Recht bekommen)*	He's such a nice boy. He doesn't ~ to be made fun of.
	workplace [ˈwɜːkpleɪs]	Arbeitsplatz	
	(to) **yell** [jel]	schreien	(to) shout loudly "Careful," she **~ed.**
	(to) **avoid** sth./ (to) **avoid** doing sth. [əˈvɔɪd]	etwas vermeiden / vermeiden, etwas zu tun	This area is dangerous and should be **~ed.** Keeping active in winter helps you to ~ getting a cold.
	gossip [ˈgɒsɪp]	Klatsch, Tratsch	noun: **gossip** – verb: (to) **gossip** (klatschen, tratschen)
	appropriate [əˈprəʊpriət]	angemessen, passend, geeignet	It's important to wear ~ clothes for a job interview.
	comprehension [ˌkɒmprɪˈhenʃn]	Verständnis	To check your ~ you can answer these questions. (F) la compréhension (L) comprehendere (*verstehen*)

	analysis [ə'næləsɪs], *pl* **analyses** [ə'næləsiːz]	Analyse, Auswertung	noun: **analysis** [ə'næləsɪs] – verb: (to) **analyse** ['ænəlaɪz] (*AE:* (to) **analyze)** (analysieren, auswerten, untersuchen) (F) l'analyse (*f*)
	critical ['krɪtɪkl]	kritisch	She made some ~ comments in an interview. Our English teacher is always very ~ of our work.
p. 88	**illustration** [ˌɪlə'streɪʃn]	Illustration, Abbildung	Sometimes a photo or an ~ can help you to understand a new word.
	effective [ɪ'fektɪv]	effektiv, wirkungsvoll	! stress: **effective** [ɪ'fektɪv] noun: **effect** ((Aus-)Wirkung) – adj: **effective** (F) efficere (*bewirken*)
	reference (to) ['refrəns]	Verweis (auf), Bezug (auf)	noun: **reference** ['refrəns] – verb: (to) **refer to** [rɪ'fɜː] (verweisen auf; sich beziehen auf)
	detailed ['diːteɪld]	ausführlich, detailliert	Can you give a ~ description of the person who attacked you? (F) détaillé, e
	(to) **be mistaken** [mɪ'steɪkən]	sich irren, sich täuschen	Bob and Joan are cousins, if **I'm** not ~. (= if I'm not wrong; if I have understood correctly)

Unit 4 New Zealand

pp. 90/91	**mysterious** [mɪ'stɪəriəs]	mysteriös, geheimnisvoll	! stress: **mys<u>te</u>rious** [mɪ'stɪəriəs] (F) mystérieux, se (L) mysterium
	awe-inspiring ['ɔː‿ɪnspaɪərɪŋ]	erfurchtgebietend	an ~-~ building/piece of music = a building/piece of music that you admire because it is so impressive
	development [dɪ'veləpmənt]	Entwicklung	verb: (to) **develop** – noun: **development**
	Māori ['maʊri]	Maori *(Ureinwohner/in Neuseelands);* maorisch	
	ancestor ['ænsestə]	Vorfahr/in	Our **~s** lived much shorter lives than we do.
	other-worldly [ˌʌðə 'wɜːldli]	(welt)entrückt; überirdisch *(nicht von dieser Welt)*	The song creates an almost ~-~ atmosphere.
	landscape ['lændskeɪp]	Landschaft	
	beauty ['bjuːti]	Schönheit	adj: **beautiful** – noun: **beauty** (F) la beauté
	craft [krɑːft]	Können, Kunst; (Kunst-)Handwerk	I'd like to learn a ~ like woodworking.
	farmland ['fɑːmlænd]	Ackerland; landwirtschaftlich genutzte Fläche	land used for farming
	chanting ['tʃɑːntɪŋ]	(Sprech-)Gesang	verb: (to) **chant** (singen *(Sprechgesang);* skandieren) – noun: **chanting**
	surrounded by [sə'raʊndɪd]	umgeben von	The lake was ~ **by** trees and bushes.

the Pacific Ocean [pəˌsɪfɪk‿ˈəʊʃn]	der Pazifische Ozean	**the Pacific Ocean** – **the Atlantic Ocean** [ətˌlæntɪk‿ˈəʊʃn]
(to) **greet** sb. [griːt]	jn. begrüßen	When we arrived, we were **~ed** by the head teacher.
relative [ˈrelətɪv]	Verwandte(r)	aunts, uncles, cousins and other **~s**

Part A

p. 92 **herd** [hɜːd]	Herde	a **herd** of cows **at pasture** 
pasture [ˈpɑːstʃə]	Weide	
solar energy [ˌsəʊlər‿ˈenədʒi]	Solarenergie, Sonnenenergie	
battery [ˈbætəri]	Batterie, Akku	! stress: **<u>bat</u>tery** [ˈbætəri] (F) la batterie 
(to) **power** [ˈpaʊə]	antreiben, betreiben, mit Energie versorgen	The company wants to develop a solar-**~ed** car. noun: **power** – verb: (to) **power**
organic certification [ɔːˌgænɪk sɜːtɪfɪˈkeɪʃn]	*etwa:* Bio-Zertifizierung	

calf, *pl* **calves** [kɑːf, kɑːvz]	Kalb; Wade	❗ **calf = 1.** Kalb **2.** Wade 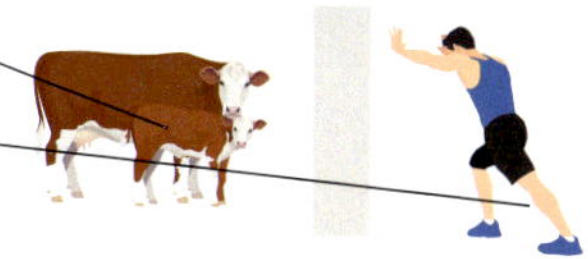
grub [ɡrʌb] *(infml)*	Essen	an informal word for **food**
gift [ɡɪft]	Geschenk; Gabe	She has a ~ for understanding things very quickly.
(to) **reduce (to)** [rɪ'djuːs]	reduzieren, verkleinern (auf)	Oh look, they have ~**d** the price. (F) réduire verb: (to) **reduce** – noun: **reduction** [rɪ'dʌkʃn] (Reduzierung, Verkleinerung, Verringerung) 
chemical ['kemɪkl]	Chemikalie	
cooperation [kəʊˌɒpə'reɪʃn]	Zusammenarbeit	doing sth. together, working together
waste [weɪst]	Abfall, Müll	

waste – (to) waste sth.

- **waste** (noun) — **1. Abfall, Müll** – You shouldn't put batteries into your household **waste.**
  2. Verschwendung – The meal at that restaurant was awful – a **waste** of time and money.
- (to) **waste** sth. **(on)** — **etwas verschwenden, vergeuden (für)** – Water is limited. Don't **waste** it.

	pollution [pə'luːʃn]	Umweltverschmutzung	Ⓕ la pollution
	calendar ['kælɪndə]	Kalender	There's a huge ~ with photos of famous buildings on our kitchen wall.
p. 93	**economy** [ɪ'kɒnəmi]	(Volks-)Wirtschaft, Ökonomie	Ⓕ l'économie (*f*)
	agriculture ['ægrɪkʌltʃə]	Landwirtschaft	Ⓕ l'agriculture f Ⓛ agricultura
	(to) **export** [ɪk'spɔːt]	ausführen, exportieren	! • verb: (to) **export** [ɪk'spɔːt] ◄► (to) **import** [ɪm'pɔːt] – • noun: **export** ['ekspɔːt] ◄► **import** ['ɪmpɔːt]
	goods *(pl)* [gʊdz]	Waren, Güter	(to) produce/buy/sell/export/import **goods**
	globalization (*BE auch:* **globalisation)** [ˌgləʊbəlaɪ'zeɪʃn]	Globalisierung	noun: **globalization, globalisation** – adj: **global** ['gləʊbl] (global) **global warming** (Erderwärmung)
	tourism ['tʊərɪzəm, 'tɔːrɪzəm]	Tourismus	Ⓕ le tourisme
	valuable ['væljuəbl]	wertvoll	verb: (to) **value** – noun: **value** – adj: **valuable**

reputation [ˌrepju'teɪʃn]	Ruf, Reputation	(to) have a good/bad ~ his ~ as a friendly/helpful/tolerant person
once again	erneut, wieder (einmal), einmal mehr	This shows **once** ~ how important it is to make the right career choices.
intensive [ɪn'tensɪv]	intensiv	~ farming; an ~ language course; ~ training; an ~ discussion adj: **intensive** – verb: (to) **intensify** [ɪn'tensɪfaɪ] (verstärken, intensivieren) – noun: **intensification** [ɪnˌtensɪfɪ'keɪʃn] (Verstärkung, Intensivierung)
wetland ['wetlənd], *auch:* **wetlands** *(pl)*	Feuchtgebiet(e), Sumpfgebiet(e)	
(to) **drain** [dreɪn]	entwässern, trockenlegen	(to) make empty or dry; (to) become empty or dry They want to try to ~ the swamp/the wetlands.
(to) **warn** sb. [wɔːn]	jn. warnen	*English:* (to) **warn sb. not to do** sth. *German:* **jn. davor warnen, etwas zu tun** My parents **~ed me not to walk** home alone.
openness ['əʊpənnəs]	Offenheit, Aufgeschlossenheit	His ~ about his problems surprised us. We need a new ~ to change and renewal.

	trade [treɪd]	Handel	• noun: **trade** – • verb: (to) **trade** (Handel treiben; (ein)tauschen) Germany **~s** a lot with China. He **~d** his sweets for a toy car. (L) tradere (*übergeben*)
	(to) **pose a risk/a problem** [pəʊz]	ein Risiko/ein Problem darstellen	Too much fast food **~s a risk** to your health.
	drastic ['dræstɪk]	drastisch	~ changes; ~ effects; a ~ rise in temperature
	(to) **recover (from)** [rɪ'kʌvə]	sich erholen (von)	It takes between 3 and 7 days to ~ **from** a cold. (L) recuperare (*wiedererlangen*)
	greenhouse gas [ˌgriːnhaʊs 'gæs]	Treibhausgas	The gases that cause global warming are called ~ **gases.**
	CO_2 (carbon dioxide) [ˌkɑːbən daɪ'ɒksaɪd]	Kohlendioxid	one of the greenhouse gases
p. 94	**item** ['aɪtəm]	Posten, Artikel, Punkt *(auf einer Liste)*	one thing on a list of things to do, talk about, etc. The second ~ on tonight's news was a report about the situation in Afghanistan.
	category [*BE* 'kætəgəri, *AE* 'kætəgɔːri]	Kategorie	! stress: **category** ['kætəgəri] (F) la catégorie

	penguin ['peŋgwɪn]	Pinguin	**penguins** 
p. 95	**grocery** ['grəʊsəri] (*AE meist:* **grocery store**)	Lebensmittelgeschäft	! **groceries** *(pl)* = Lebensmittel I need to get some cheese and eggs and other **groceries.**
	(to) **book** [bʊk]	buchen, reservieren	That restaurant is always full. You'll need to ~ a table.
	flexible ['fleksəbl]	flexibel	He hates change. He's not very ~. ! stress: **<u>fle</u>xible** ['fleksəbl]
p. 96	**shortly** ['ʃɔːtli]	in Kürze, bald; kurz, gleich	! **shortly** = **1.** soon – Tickets will be available ~. **2.** not long – We came home ~ after midnight.
	passenger ['pæsɪndʒə]	Passagier/in, Fahrgast, Fluggast	
	(to) **fasten** sth. ['fɑːsn]	etwas zumachen, festmachen, befestigen	The rope is **fastened** to a tree. 
	seatbelt ['siːtbelt] (*auch:* **seat belt**)	Sicherheitsgurt	**Fasten your seatbelt.** 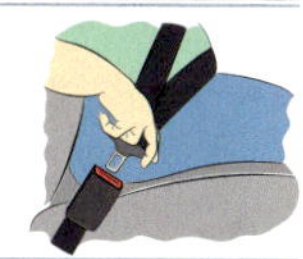

	marvellous ['mɑːvələs] (*AE:* **marvelous**)	wunderbar, fabelhaft	extremely good, wonderful, fantastic
	kindergarten ['kɪndəgɑːtn]	*BE:* Kindergarten; *AE:* Vorschule	
p. 97	**involvement (in)** [ɪn'vɒlvmənt]	Engagement (für); Beteiligung (an)	(L) involvere *(hineinwickeln)*

involvement

involvement (in)	His **involvement** in the peace movement made him famous.	Engagement (für); Beteiligung (an)
(to) **get involved (in)**	At university, she **got involved in** a theatre group.	sich engagieren (für, bei); sich beteiligen (an)
(to) **be involved (in)**	We **have been involved in** our local church for six years.	etwas zu tun haben (mit); beteiligt sein (an)

activist ['æktɪvɪst]	Aktivist/in	! stress: **<u>act</u>ivist** ['æktɪvɪst] (F) l'activiste *(m, f)* (L) agere, actum *(tun, bewegen, handeln)*
campaign [kæm'peɪn]	Kampagne	noun: **a campaign for/against** sth. verb: (to) **campaign for/against** sth. (sich einsetzen, kämpfen für/gegen)
cause [kɔːz]	Anliegen, Sache, Zweck	We're trying to raise money for a good ~. (L) causa ! **cause** = **1.** Ursache; **2.** Anliegen, Sache, Zweck

citizen ['sɪtɪzn]	(Staats-)Bürger/in	Mr Evans has applied to become a German ~. (F) le citoyen, la citoyenne (L) civis, is m/f
democracy [dɪ'mɒkrəsi]	Demokratie	! stress: **de<u>mo</u>cracy** [dɪ'mɒkrəsi] (F) la démocratie
opinion poll [ə'pɪnjən pəʊl]	Meinungsumfrage	(L) opinio, onis *f* (*Meinung*)
petition [pə'tɪʃn]	Petition, Eingabe, Unterschriftensammlung	! stress: **pe<u>ti</u>tion** [pə'tɪʃn] (F) la pétition (L) petere (*zu erreichen suchen*)
party ['pɑːti]	Partei	(F) le parti
policy ['pɒləsi]	Politik *(politische Linie)*, Richtlinie(n)	

German "Politik"

1. *(politisches Leben, Geschehen)* **politics** *(no pl)* – Are you interested in **politics?**
2. *(politische Linie)* **policy** – What is your party's **policy** on education? – What is the company **policy** on working from home?

pressure group ['preʃə gruːp]	Pressuregroup, Lobby	(L) premere, pressum (*drücken*)
referendum [ˌrefə'rendəm], *pl* **referendums, referenda**	Volksentscheid	

signature [ˈsɪgnətʃə]	Unterschrift	 He's **signing** a letter. (F) la signature – signer (L) signare (*versiegeln, mit einem Zeichen versehen*)
(to) **demand** [dɪˈmɑːnd]	fordern, verlangen	The workers **~ed** more money. (F) demander verb: (to) **demand** – noun: **demand** (Forderung)
(to) **elect** sb. [ɪˈlekt]	jn. wählen	We're going to ~ a new government in autumn. *English:* She **was elected president.** *German:* Sie **wurde zur Präsidentin gewählt.** verb: (to) **elect** – noun: **election** [ɪˈlekʃn] (Wahl) (L) eligere, electum (*auswählen*)
banner [ˈbænə]	Spruchband	The protesters carried **~s** with the slogan "Stop it now".
investment [ɪnˈvestmənt]	Investition, (Geld-)Anlage	verb: (to) **invest in** [ɪnˈvest] (investieren in) – noun: **investment**
MP [ˌemˈpiː] **(= Member of Parliament)**	Parlamentsmitglied, Abgeordnete(r)	*in Britain:* **MP** (Member of Parliament) *in Germany:* **MdB** (Mitglied des Deutschen Bundestags)

	sexism ['seksɪzəm]	Sexismus	! adj: **sexist** ['seksɪst] (sexistisch) noun: **sexism** ['seksɪzəm]
	crime [kraɪm]	Verbrechen; Kriminalität	The worst ~ is murder, I think. In most cities, ~ is a big problem. (F) le crime (L) crimen, inis n
	mental health [ˌmentl 'helθ]	psychische Gesundheit	
	recycling [ˌriː'saɪklɪŋ]	Recycling, Wiederverwertung	verb: (to) **recycle** [ˌriː'saɪkl] – noun: **recycling**
p. 101	**accommodation** *(no pl)* [əˌkɒmə'deɪʃn]	Unterkunft	We like to stay at a nice hotel when we're on holiday. What kind of ~ do you prefer?
	excursion [ɪk'skɜːʃn]	Ausflug, Exkursion	a short journey made for pleasure
	(to) **go hiking** ['haɪkɪŋ]	(berg)wandern gehen	(to) go for long walks in the country
	itinerary [aɪ'tɪnərəri]	Reiseroute	We'll probably travel through Europe next year but still need to plan our ~.
	luggage ['lʌgɪdʒ] *(bes. BE)*, **baggage** ['bægɪdʒ] *(bes. AE)*	Gepäck	
	suitcase ['suːtkeɪs]	Koffer	
	(to) **go sightseeing** ['saɪtsiːɪŋ]	sich Sehenswürdigkeiten ansehen	First we **went** ~ in London, and in the second week we went hiking in Wales.

sleeping bag ['sliːpɪŋ bæg]	Schlafsack	a **sleeping bag** 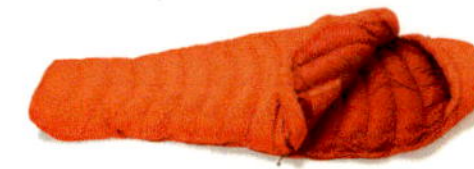
van [væn]	Transporter, Lieferwagen	a **van** 
visa ['viːzə]	Visum	You'll need a ~ if you want to travel to India.
(airport) terminal ['tɜːmɪnl]	Terminal, Abfertigungsgebäude	a building at an airport where passengers arrive/leave
flight attendant ['flaɪt‿ətendənt]	Flugbegleiter/in	 **flight attendants**
customs *(pl)* ['kʌstəmz]	Bräuche, Gebräuche, Sitten	Some foreign ~ seem strange when you first go abroad.
travel agent ['trævl‿eɪdʒnt]	Reisebürokaufmann/-frau	Dad has gone to the ~ **agent's** to buy air tickets. (= Reisebüro)

Part B

p. 102	**(to) be descended from** [dɪ'sendɪd]	abstammen von	He says he **is ~ from** an Indian king.
	tribe [traɪb]	(Volks-)Stamm	
	resources *(pl)* [rɪ'sɔːsɪz, rɪ'zɔːsɪz]	Mittel, Ressourcen	
	common ['kɒmən]	gemeinsame(r, s)	! **common** = **1.** häufig; weit verbreitet – Olivia is a very **common** name in Britain. **2.** gemeinsame(r, s) – Germany and Austria have a **common** language. (L) communis, -e (*allgemein*)
	identity [aɪ'dentəti]	Identität	! stress: **<u>iden</u>tity** [aɪ'dentəti] (F) l'identité (*f*) (L) idem (*derselbe*)
	concept ['kɒnsept]	Vorstellung, Begriff, Konzept	I find it difficult to talk about abstract **~s** in English.
	(to) **pass** sth. **on (to** sb.**)** [ˌpɑːs‿'ɒn]	etwas weitergeben (an jn.)	If you give sth. to sb. else (after you have received it or used it yourself), you **~ it on to sb.** Can you **~ on** the message **to** your boss, please?
	settlement ['setlmənt]	Siedlung	verb: (to) **settle** – nouns: **settlement;** *(person)* **settler**

gun [gʌn]	Schusswaffe	several **guns** 
cannon ['kænən], *pl* **cannon, cannons**	Kanone, Geschütz	a **cannon** 
disease [dɪ'ziːz]	*(ansteckende)* Krankheit	! • **disease** wird für ansteckende oder sehr ernsthafte Erkrankungen verwendet: She has a blood **disease.** Thousands of trees died from **disease.** • Das allgemeinere Wort für „Krankheit“ ist **illness:** After a week of **illness,** she went back to school.
weapon ['wepən]	Waffe	The police found guns, knives and other **~s** in his house.
devastation [ˌdevə'steɪʃn]	Verwüstung, Zerstörung	The floods caused widespread **~.** (= verheerende/weitreichende Verwüstung(en)/Zerstörung)
livestock ['laɪvstɒk]	Vieh, Nutztiere	farm animals like cows or sheep

extinction [ɪk'stɪŋkʃn]	Aussterben	Lots of plants and animals are in danger of **~**. (= they might die out) adj: **extinct** [ɪk'stɪŋkt] (ausgestorben) – noun: **extinction**
treaty ['triːti]	Vertrag, Abkommen	a formal agreement between two or more countries
empire ['empaɪə]	Reich, Imperium	(F) l'empire *(m)*
violent ['vaɪələnt]	gewalttätig; gewaltsam	(F) violent,e (L) violentus
disagreement [ˌdɪsə'griːmənt]	Uneinigkeit, Zerwürfnis, Streit	a situation where people argue about sth. or have different opinions about sth.
battle ['bætl]	Schlacht; Kampf	a fight between armies; a violent fight between groups of people
society [sə'saɪəti]	(die) Gesellschaft	*No article:* **in (modern) society** **in der (modernen) Gesellschaft** (F) la société (L) societas
(to) **govern** ['gʌvən]	regieren	verb: (to) **govern** – noun: **government** (F) gouverner
majority [mə'dʒɒrəti]	Mehrheit	There are 16 girls and 13 boys in my class. The girls are in the **~**. **majority** ◄► **minority** [maɪ'nɒrəti] (Minderheit)
(to) **result in** sth. [rɪ'zʌlt]	zu etwas führen, etwas zur Folge haben	The war **~ed in** millions of deaths.

	poverty ['pɒvəti]	Armut	adj: **poor** – noun: **poverty**
	level ['levl]	Grad, Niveau; (Lern-)Stand	Lower speed limits might reduce the ~ of noise. What ~ is this course, beginners' or advanced?
	defence [dɪ'fens] (*AE:* **defense)**	Verteidigung	verb: (to) **defend** – noun: **defence** Find arguments in ~ of your position. (… zur Verteidigung deiner Position)
	(to) **punish** ['pʌnɪʃ]	bestrafen	verb: (to) **punish** – noun: **punishment**
	officially [ə'fɪʃəli]	offiziell	adj: **official** – adv: **officially** **officially** ◄► **unofficially** [ˌʌnə'fɪʃəli] (inoffiziell)
	mistreatment [ˌmɪs'triːtmənt]	Misshandlung	verb: (to) **treat** [triːt] (behandeln) – We should **treat** other people with respect. nouns: **treatment; mistreatment**
	politician [ˌpɒlə'tɪʃn]	Politiker/in	! stress and pronunciation: **politics** ['pɒlətɪks] – **political** [pə'lɪtɪkl] – **politician** [ˌpɒlə'tɪʃn] (F) le politicien, la politicienne (L) politicus, a, um (*politisch*)
p. 103	**interviewee** [ˌɪntəvjuː'iː]	Interviewpartner/in, Befragte(r)	**interviewer** = the person who asks the questions in an interview **interviewee** = the person who answers the questions
	journalist ['dʒɜːnəlɪst]	Journalist/in	sb. who writes news stories for newspapers, TV, etc.

	(to) **deliver** [dɪ'lɪvə]	zustellen, überbringen	! (to) **deliver** = **1.** liefern, ausliefern *(Waren, Essen, …)* **2.** zustellen, überbringen *(Nachricht, Botschaft, …)*
	multi- ['mʌlti]	multi, Multi; viel-, mehr-	**multi**-cultural; **multi**-coloured; **multi**-lingual (*auch:* **multi**cultural; **multi**coloured; **multi**lingual) a **multi**-millionaire (L) multus
	(to) **unite** [ju'naɪt]	(sich) vereinen, vereinigen	
p. 104	(to) **separate** ['sepəreɪt]	trennen	! adj: **separate** ['seprət] (getrennt) adv: **separately** ['seprətli] (einzeln, separat) verb: (to) **separate** ['sepəreɪt] (F) séparer (L) separare
	rotten ['rɒtn]	verfault, faul, verdorben	I hate the smell of ~ meat.
	at risk [rɪsk]	in Gefahr, gefährdet	Lots of plants and animals are **at** ~ of dying out. (= in danger of dying out) With Covid-19, old people are more **at** ~ than others.
	priest [priːst]	Priester/in	
	(to) **communicate (with)** [kə'mjuːnɪkeɪt]	kommunizieren (mit), sich verständigen (mit)	If you want to ~ **with** foreigners, the best thing to do is learn their language. (F) communiquer (L) communicare
p. 105	(to) **amaze sb.** [ə'meɪz]	jn. erstaunen, verblüffen	adj: **amazing** – verb: (to) **amaze**
	on behalf of sb. / **on** sb.'s **behalf** [bɪ'hɑːf]	im Namen/im Auftrag von jm.; für jn.	I would like to thank you **on** ~ **of** the whole school. Mr Carter signed the document **on his son's** ~.

	brief [bri:f]	kurz (gefasst), knapp, von kurzer Dauer	Please be ~. / Make it ~, please. (Fasse dich kurz, bitte.) He died after a ~ illness at the age of 33. (F) bref, brève (L) brevis
	feature ['fi:tʃə]	Merkmal, Eigenschaft, Kennzeichen	something important, interesting or typical of a place or thing
	(to) **commemorate** sth. [kə'meməreɪt]	einer Sache gedenken, an etwas erinnern	The family came together to ~ the anniversary of John's death.
	(to) **found** [faʊnd]	gründen	The company was ~**ed** in 1884. ! *regular:* (to) **found** – **founded** – **founded** (gründen) *irregular:* (to) **find** – **found** – **found** (finden)
p. 106	(to) **scratch** [skrætʃ]	kratzen	*English:* He **scratched his head/foot.** *German:* Er **kratzte sich am Kopf/Fuß.**
	feast [fi:st]	Festessen	Everyone was busy preparing the Christmas ~.
	(to) **heat** [hi:t]	erhitzen; heizen	verb: (to) **heat** – noun: **heat** (Hitze)
	volcanic [vɒl'kænɪk]	vulkanisch	adj: **volcanic** – noun: **volcano** [vɒl'keɪnəʊ], *pl* **volcanoes, volcanos** (Vulkan)
	pit [pɪt]	Grube	a large deep hole in the ground

	(to) **gather** ['gæðə]	(sich) versammeln	(to) come together; (to) bring together In the evening, we all **~ed** around the campfire.
	open-minded [ˌəʊpən 'maɪndɪd]	aufgeschlossen, unvoreingenommen	When you're travelling, you need to be positive and **open-~.**
	backyard [ˌbæk'jɑːd]	*BE:* Hinterhof; *AE:* Garten hinter dem Haus	
	mammal ['mæml]	Säugetier	
	(to) **litter** ['lɪtə]	Abfälle zurücklassen *(Müll einfach wegwerfen)*	verb: (to) **litter** – noun: **litter** (Abfall)
	wolf [wʊlf], *pl* **wolves** [wʊlvz]	Wolf	a **wolf** 
p. 107	**series,** *pl* **series** ['sɪəriːz]	(Sende-)Reihe, Serie	What's your favourite ~ ? Do you watch it every week? (F) la série (L) series f
	useful ['juːsfl]	nützlich	This map is very ~ for finding your way around town. (L) usus
	unknown [ˌʌn'nəʊn]	unbekannt, nicht bekannt	not known

p. 109	(to) **examine** [ɪg'zæmɪn]	untersuchen	I had a bad headache, so the doctor **~d** me. (F) examiner (L) examinare
	(to) **address** sb. [ə'dres]	zu jm. sprechen; jn. ansprechen; das Wort an jn. richten	(to) **address** an audience/a meeting
	logical ['lɒdʒɪkl]	logisch	**logical ◄► illogical** [ɪ'lɒdʒɪkl] (unlogisch) (F) logique – illogique (L) logicus, a, um
	appeal (to) [ə'piːl]	Appell, Aufruf (an)	The police made an ~ to the public, asking for information. ! spelling: *(English)* **appeal** – *(German)* **Appell**
	explanation [ˌeksplə'neɪʃn]	Erklärung	verb: (to) **explain** – noun: **explanation**
	rather (…) than ['rɑːðə ðæn, 'rɑːðə ðən]	eher (…) als, lieber (…) als, statt	I'd **rather** walk ~ pay for a taxi. My grandma used to say that children should be seen **rather** ~ heard.
	delivery [dɪ'lɪvəri]	Vortrag(sweise)	the way you say something Sometimes your ~ can be more important than the content of your speech.
	impact ['ɪmpækt]	Auswirkung, Effekt	Sometimes your delivery can have a stronger ~ than the content of your speech.
	alliteration [əˌlɪtə'reɪʃn]	Alliteration, Stabreim, Anlautreim	the use of words that begin with the same sound: **B**etty **B**otter **b**ought some **b**utter.

repetition [ˌrepəˈtɪʃn]	Wiederholung	verb: (to) **repeat** – noun: **repetition** (F) la répétition (L) repetitio

Part C

p. 110 **throughout …** [θruːˈaʊt]	überall in …, in ganz …	! **throughout** = 1. *(örtlich)* **throughout Europe/the world** in ganz Europa/in der ganzen Welt; europaweit/weltweit 2. *(zeitlich)* **throughout the year** das ganze Jahr hindurch
lingua franca [ˌlɪŋgwə ˈfræŋkə]	Verkehrssprache, Lingua franca	a language that is used by speakers of different languages to talk to each other
diplomacy [dɪˈpləʊməsi]	Diplomatie	! stress: **diplomacy** [dɪˈpləʊməsi] (F) la diplomatie
(to) **get a message across**	eine Botschaft rüberbringen, sich verständlich machen	It might be a good idea to add some illustrations to your presentation in order to **get your ~ across.**
(to) **depend on** [dɪˈpend]	abhängen von; angewiesen sein auf	We go by bike sometimes – it **~s on** the weather. As we live in a village, we ~ **on** the car to get around. (F) dépendre (L) dependere
usage [ˈjuːsɪdʒ, ˈjuːzɪdʒ]	Gebrauch *(insbes. Sprachgebrauch)*	He has written an interesting article on the ~ of the words *illness* and *disease.*

bill [bɪl]	Rechnung	*English:* **Can I have the bill, please?** *German:* **Die Rechnung, bitte. / Zahlen, bitte.**
(to) **colonize** ['kɒlənaɪz] (*BE auch:* (to) **colonise**)	besiedeln, kolonisieren	in 1884, Germany began to ~ parts of Africa.
widespread ['waɪdspred]	weit verbreitet, groß(flächig)	There have been reports of ~ flooding. The floods caused ~ damage to houses and buildings.
(to) **contribute** sth. **(to)** [kən'trɪbjuːt]	etwas beitragen, beisteuern (zu)	He's too shy and doesn't ~ much **to** class discussions. (F) contribuer (L) contribuere
mostly ['məʊstli]	hauptsächlich, überwiegend, meistens	The milk we drink is ~ from cows.
scholar ['skɒlə]	Gelehrte(r), Wissenschaftler/in	sb. who knows a lot about a subject because they have studied it in detail
(to) **discourage** [dɪs'kʌrɪdʒ]	unterbinden, zu verhindern suchen; abschrecken	· (to) **discourage** smoking/drug use (to) **discourage** thieves/criminals · (to) **discourage sb. from doing** sth. (jn. davon abhalten, etwas zu tun) – Her parents tried to ~ **her from leaving** the country. (to) **encourage** ◄► (to) **discourage**
(to) **dominate** ['dɒmɪneɪt]	dominieren, beherrschen	Do you think that American culture hast started to ~ the world?

globe [gləʊb]	Welt, Erdball; Globus; Kugel	❗ **globe** = **1.** another word for **world** **2.** a kind of ball with a map of the world on it **3.** a thing that is like a ball in shape
difficulty ['dɪfɪkəlti]	Schwierigkeit(en)	adj: **difficult** – noun: **difficulty** (F) la difficulté (L) difficultas
(to) **slow down** [ˌsləʊ 'daʊn]	langsamer werden; (sich) verlangsamen	You speak so fast that I can't understand you! Please can you ~ **down** a bit?
p. 111 **quality** ['kwɒləti]	Eigenschaft, Qualität	❗ stress: **quality** ['kwɒləti] **a high-quality translation** = eine qualitativ hochwertige Übersetzung (F) la qualité (L) qualis (*wie beschaffen?*)
tool [tuːl]	Werkzeug; (Hilfs-)Mittel	 some **tools**
translator [trænz'leɪtə]	Übersetzer/in	sb. who translates into a different language

(to) **replace** sb./sth. **(with)** [rɪ'pleɪs]	jn./etwas ersetzen (durch); austauschen	In this exercise, you have to ~ all the nouns **with** pronouns. (F) remplacer
unlike [ˌʌn'laɪk]	im Gegensatz zu	I'm not a good swimmer, ~ my sister. She swims like a fish. **like ◄► unlike**
chunk [tʃʌŋk]	(dickes, großes) Stück	a **chunk** of cheese 
entire [ɪn'taɪə]	ganze(r, s)	the ~ world = the whole world (F) entier, entière · adj: **entire** · adv: **entirely** [ɪn'taɪəli] (völlig, gänzlich) **entirely** new/possible/different/unexpected
instantly ['ɪnstəntli]	sofort	= immediately
(to) **access** sth. ['ækses]	auf etwas zugreifen	verb: (to) **access** – noun: **access** – adj: **accessible** [ək'sesəbl] (zugänglich, erreichbar)
linguistics [lɪŋ'gwɪstɪks]	Sprachwissenschaft, Linguistik	
cross-cultural [ˌkrɒs 'kʌltʃərəl]	interkulturell	

complex ['kɒmpleks]	komplex	**a complex sentence** (= Satzgefüge aus Haupt- und Nebensatz) ! stress: **complex** ['kɒmpleks]
handy ['hændi] *(infml)*	nützlich, praktisch, hilfreich; griffbereit, zur Hand; geschickt	· The following tips might **come in ~:** … (… könnten sich als **nützlich** erweisen) · Have you got a knife ~ ? (**griffbereit, zur Hand**) · She's really ~ with her computer. (**geschickt**) ! false friends: *German* **Handy** = *BE:* **mobile (phone),** *AE:* **cell (phone)**
skilled [skɪld]	geschickt	He's very ~ at cooking and baking.
(to) **relate** sth. **to** sth. [rɪ'leɪt]	etwas mit etwas verknüpfen, etwas zu etwas in Beziehung setzen	A good translator must be able to ~ words **to** the context.
tone [təʊn]	Ton	You could tell he was nervous from the ~ of his voice. (L) tonus
poetic [pəʊ'etɪk]	poetisch	adj: **poetic** – noun: **poem** (Gedicht)
sarcastic [sɑː'kæstɪk]	sarkastisch	
essay ['eseɪ]	Aufsatz	a short piece of writing by a student
p. 112 **interruption** [ˌɪntə'rʌpʃn]	Unterbrechung	verb: (to) **interrupt** – noun: **interruption**

	(to) **rehearse** [rɪ'hɜːs]	proben; einüben *(sich leise vorsprechen)*	Next week we're going to start **rehearsing** for the school play.
p. 113	**faraway** ['fɑːrəweɪ]	fern, abgelegen, entlegen	**faraway** countries
	(to) **transport** [træn'spɔːt]	transportieren, befördern	! verb: (to) **transport** [træn'spɔːt] – noun: **transport** ['trænspɔːt]
	fossil fuel ['fɒsl fjuːəl]	fossiler Brennstoff	Oil, petrol, gas and coal are all fossil **~s**.
p. 114	**tournament** ['tʊənəmənt, 'tɔːnəmənt]	Turnier, Wettkampf	a competition

Access to cultures: Giving compliments

p. 118	**compliment** ['kɒmplɪmənt]	Kompliment	! stress: **compliment** ['kɒmplɪmənt] *English:* (to) **give** / (to) **pay** **sb. a compliment** *German:* **jm. ein Kompliment machen** (F) le compliment
	bandage ['bændɪdʒ]	Bandage, Verband	He's got a **bandage** on his head. (F) le bandage 

	sling [slɪŋ]	Schlinge	He has his arm in a **sling.** 
	vase [*BE:* vɑːz, *AE:* veɪs, veɪz]	Vase	a **vase** of flowers (F) le vase 
	monitor ['mɒnɪtə]	Monitor, Bildschirm	
	buddy ['bʌdi] *(infml)*	Kumpel, Freund/in	
p. 119	**thoughtful** ['θɔːtfl]	nachdenklich	He looked ~ for a moment, and then began to explain. noun: **thought** – adj: **thoughtful**

Irregular verbs

infinitive	simple past	past participle	
(to) **be**	**was; were**	**been**	sein
(to) **beat**	**beat**	**beaten**	schlagen; besiegen
(to) **become**	**became**	**become**	werden
(to) **begin**	**began**	**begun**	beginnen, anfangen
(to) **bend**	**bent**	**bent**	sich bücken, sich beugen
(to) **bite** [aɪ]	**bit** [ɪ]	**bitten** [ɪ]	beißen
(to) **blow sth. out**	**blew**	**blown**	etwas auspusten, ausblasen
(to) **break** [eɪ]	**broke**	**broken**	brechen; zerbrechen
(to) **bring**	**brought**	**brought**	(mit-, her)bringen
(to) **build**	**built**	**built**	bauen
(to) **burst** into tears	**burst**	**burst**	in Tränen ausbrechen
(to) **buy**	**bought**	**bought**	kaufen
(to) **catch**	**caught**	**caught**	fangen
(to) **choose** [uː]	**chose** [əʊ]	**chosen** [əʊ]	aussuchen, (aus)wählen; sich aussuchen
(to) **come**	**came**	**come**	kommen
(to) **cost**	**cost**	**cost**	kosten
(to) **cut**	**cut**	**cut**	schneiden
(to) **dig**	**dug**	**dug**	graben
(to) **do**	**did**	**done** [ʌ]	tun, machen

infinitive	simple past	past participle	
(to) **draw**	**drew**	**drawn**	zeichnen
(to) **drive** [aɪ]	**drove** [əʊ]	**driven** [ɪ]	(mit dem Auto) fahren
(to) **drink**	**drank**	**drunk**	trinken
(to) **eat**	**ate** [et, eɪt]	**eaten**	essen
(to) **fall**	**fell**	**fallen**	fallen, stürzen; hinfallen
(to) **feed**	**fed**	**fed**	füttern; sich ernähren
(to) **feel**	**felt**	**felt**	fühlen; sich fühlen
(to) **fight**	**fought**	**fought**	(be)kämpfen
(to) **find**	**found**	**found**	finden
(to) **fly**	**flew**	**flown**	fliegen
(to) **forget**	**forgot**	**forgotten**	vergessen
(to) **freeze**	**froze**	**frozen**	(ge)frieren; zufrieren; einfrieren
(to) **get**	**got**	**got**	bekommen; holen; werden; gelangen
(to) **give**	**gave**	**given**	geben
(to) **go**	**went**	**gone** [ɒ]	gehen
(to) **grow**	**grew**	**grown**	wachsen; anbauen, anpflanzen
(to) **hang**	**hung**	**hung**	hängen
(to) **have**	**had**	**had**	haben
(to) **hear** [ɪə]	**heard** [ɜː]	**heard** [ɜː]	hören

infinitive	simple past	past participle	
(to) **hide** [aɪ]	**hid** [ɪ]	**hidden** [ɪ]	verstecken; sich verstecken
(to) **hit**	**hit**	**hit**	schlagen
(to) **hold**	**held**	**held**	halten; abhalten *(Versammlung)*
(to) **hurt**	**hurt**	**hurt**	schmerzen, wehtun; verletzen
(to) **keep**	**kept**	**kept**	behalten; aufheben, aufsparen; aufbewahren
(to) **kneel** [niːl]	**knelt** [nelt]	**knelt** [nelt]	knien
(to) **know** [nəʊ]	**knew** [njuː]	**known** [nəʊn]	wissen; kennen
(to) **lead** [iː]	**led**	**led**	führen, leiten
(to) **leave** [iː]	**left**	**left**	(weg)gehen; abfahren; (zurück)lassen; verlassen
(to) **lend sb. sth.**	**lent**	**lent**	jm. etwas leihen
(to) **let**	**let**	**let**	lassen
(to) **lie**	**lay**	**lain**	liegen
(to) **light** [aɪ]	**lit** [ɪ]	**lit** [ɪ]	anzünden
(to) **lose** [uː]	**lost** [ɒ]	**lost** [ɒ]	verlieren
(to) **make**	**made**	**made**	machen; herstellen
(to) **mean** [iː]	**meant** [e]	**meant** [e]	bedeuten; meinen
(to) **meet** [iː]	**met** [e]	**met**	treffen; sich treffen; kennenlernen
(to) **pay**	**paid**	**paid**	bezahlen
(to) **put**	**put**	**put**	(etwas wohin) tun, legen, stellen

infinitive	simple past	past participle	
(to) **read** [iː]	**read** [e]	**read** [e]	lesen
(to) **ride** [aɪ]	**rode**	**ridden** [ɪ]	reiten; *(Rad)* fahren
(to) **ring**	**rang**	**rung**	klingeln, läuten
(to) **rise** [aɪ]	**rose**	**risen** [ɪ]	(an)steigen, aufsteigen; (sich) erhöhen
(to) **run**	**ran**	**run**	rennen, laufen; leiten, führen *(Hotel, Firma)*
(to) **say** [eɪ]	**said** [e]	**said** [e]	sagen
(to) **see**	**saw**	**seen**	sehen
(to) **sell**	**sold**	**sold**	verkaufen
(to) **send**	**sent**	**sent**	schicken, senden
(to) **set sth. up**	**set**	**set**	etwas errichten, aufbauen; etwas arrangieren
(to) **shake**	**shook**	**shaken**	schütteln
(to) **shine**	**shone** [*BE:* ɒ, *AE:* əʊ]	**shone** [ɒ, əʊ]	scheinen *(Sonne)*
(to) **shoot** [uː]	**shot** [ɒ]	**shot** [ɒ]	schießen; erschießen
(to) **sing**	**sang**	**sung**	singen
(to) **sit**	**sat**	**sat**	sitzen; sich setzen
(to) **sleep**	**slept**	**slept**	schlafen
(to) **speak** [iː]	**spoke**	**spoken**	sprechen
(to) **spend**	**spent**	**spent**	*(Zeit)* verbringen; *(Geld)* ausgeben
(to) **spin around**	**spun**	**spun**	sich (im Kreis) drehen; herumwirbeln

infinitive	simple past	past participle	
(to) **spread** [e]	**spread** [e]	**spread** [e]	ausbreiten, verbreiten; sich ausbreiten, verbreiten
(to) **stand**	**stood**	**stood**	stehen; sich (hin)stellen
(to) **steal**	**stole**	**stolen**	stehlen
(to) **stick**	**stuck**	**stuck**	stechen, stecken
(to) **swear** [eə]	**swore**	**sworn**	schwören
(to) **swim**	**swam**	**swum**	schwimmen
(to) **swing**	**swung**	**swung**	schwingen
(to) **take**	**took**	**taken**	(mit)nehmen; (weg-, hin)bringen; dauern
(to) **teach**	**taught**	**taught**	unterrichten, lehren
(to) **tear down** [teə]	**tore**	**torn**	abreißen
(to) **tell**	**told**	**told**	erzählen, berichten
(to) **think**	**thought**	**thought**	denken, glauben
(to) **throw**	**threw**	**thrown**	werfen
(to) **tread** [e]	**trod**	**trodden**	treten
(to) **understand**	**understood**	**understood**	verstehen
(to) **wake up**	**woke up**	**woken up**	aufwachen; (auf)wecken
(to) **wear** [eə]	**wore** [ɔː]	**worn** [ɔː]	tragen *(Kleidung)*
(to) **win**	**won** [ʌ]	**won** [ʌ]	gewinnen
(to) **write**	**wrote**	**written**	schreiben

Titelbild

Mauritius Images (Sydney Opera House: alamy stock photo/katacarix)

Illustrationen

Roland Beier, Berlin (S.13)

Bildquellen

Adobe Stock stock adobe.com (S.6 mitte: Henrik Larsson); **Shutterstock GmbH** shutterstock.com (S.7 mitte: e X p o s e, S.7 oben: Phil Date, S.7 unten: jeep2499, S.9 rechts: Miroslav Hlavko, S.9 links: tagstiles.com - S.Gruene, S.10: stockcreations, S.18: Melinda Fawver, S.19 unten: a40757, S.19 oben: Dudarev Mikhail, S.21: withGod, S.22: Grandpa, S.28 unten: Felipegsb, S.28 ob.li.: Joseph Sohm, S.28 ob.re.: Domenic Gareri, S.29 unten: Reginast777, S.29 oben: IngeBlessas, S.31: Vladimir Nenezic, S.40: Ico Maker, S.45 oben: browndogstudios, S.45 unten: Gary James Calder, S.49: BortN66, S.55: Kao-len, S.59: ValentinT, S.60: Matej Kastelic, S.68 oben: Zeljko Radojko, S.68 unten: Pretty Vectors, S.69 ob.li.: Happy Job, S.69 ob.re.: Lio putra, S.69 unten: Laura Gangi Pond, S.73 unten: Lemurik, S.73 mitte: Jose Angel Astor Rocha, S.73 oben: xolmgard, S.76: Julia Tim, S.77: sumroeng chinnapan, S.78 mitte: Zhenyakot, S.78 oben: Volodymyr_Dyrbavka, S.78 unten: Andresr, S.80 oben: WKung, S.80 mitte: Ton Bangkeaw, S.85: eihypnotic, S.89: Stock_VectorSale, S.90: azure1, S.92: StockSmartStart, S.93 oben: Luciano Cosmo, S.93 unten: Agnes Kantaruk).

English G Access
G9 Ausgabe 2019 · Band 5
Vokabeltaschenbuch

Im Auftrag des Verlages herausgegeben von
Jörg Rademacher, Mannheim

Erarbeitet von
Stella Hunger (Redaktion)

Lizenzmanagement
Sophie Dupiech

Umschlaggestaltung
hawemannundmosch, Berlin

Layout und technische Umsetzung
STRAIVE, Chennai, Indien

www.cornelsen.de

1. Auflage, 1. Druck 2022

Alle Drucke dieser Auflage sind inhaltlich unverändert und können im Unterricht nebeneinander verwendet werden.

Druck: H. Heenemann, Berlin

ISBN 978-3-06-036286-8

PEFC/04-31-1156

PEFC zertifiziert
Dieses Produkt stammt aus nachhaltig bewirtschafteten Wäldern und kontrollierten Quellen.

www.pefc.de